Class War 2016: Rhetoric and Revolution

Eric Michael Moberg, M.F.A., Ph.D.

Copyright © 2016

Prescott University Press

ISBN-13:
978-1533526335

ISBN-10:
1533526338

To Humanity

"I want what's coming to me...everything."

—David Koch, billionaire co-owner of Koch Industries and major contributor to the Tea Party and other conservative projects, such as the climate change denial industry.

Contents

Second Renaissance or Second Dark Ages

"We need not deceive ourselves that we can afford today the luxury of altruism and world—benefaction.... We should cease to talk about vague and unreal objectives such as human rights, the raising of the living standards, and democratization. The day is not far off when we are going to have to deal in straight power concepts. The less we are then hampered by idealistic slogans, the better."

—George Kennan head of U.S. State Department Policy Planning Staff, 1948.

---

80 percent of the world lives on less than $10 per day.

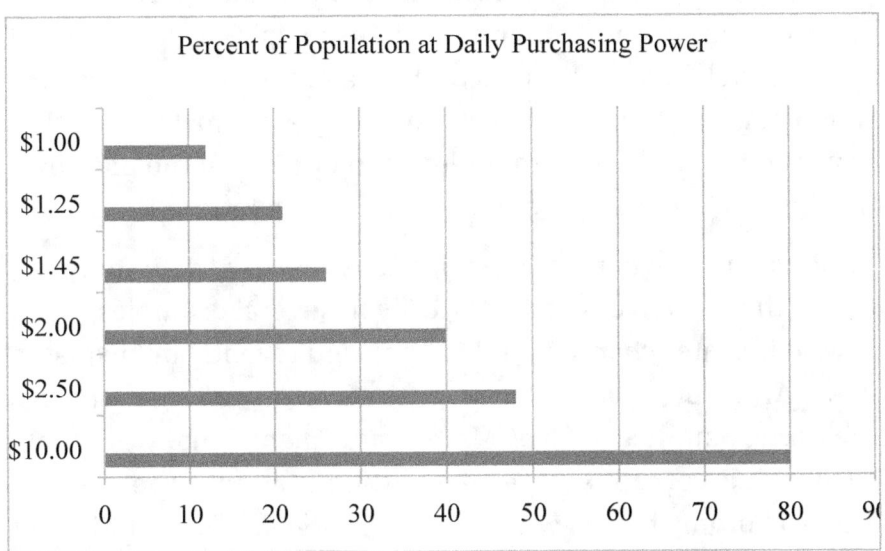

Source: World Bank

The world is on the precipice of a Second Renaissance or a Second Dark Ages. Income and, especially, wealth inequality have never been more severe, now to astronomical levels where many live on less than the price of a cappuccino a day while others amass billions, usually by manipulating or exploiting the masses, aggravating poverty and instability, and not stopping at waging wars or committing genocide for profit. The legal and illegal drug and arms trades are booming, just as speculation on the worthless derivative assets continues unabated and largely untaxed.

We are here as the result of ongoing class war waged by the ownership and ruling classes against the middle and working classes. The history of societies, nations, and empires establishing class systems so as to divide and conquer includes examples from and well before biblical times, slave trades in Africa, Europe, Asia, and the Americas, genocide of the American natives and other indigenous peoples, colonialism all over the globe that continues to this day as near as in Mexico, wars of aggression such as Vietnam, Iraq, Afghanistan, and the never ending and often fraudulent exploitation of the poor by the powers that be. The only solution is revolution.

Revolution, when successful, often follows a trichotomy model that we have seen historically in several examples covered in later chapters of this book and recently on display in the Arab Spring as well as what is currently taking shape in the Occupy and Black Lives Matter movements finally challenging corrupt American institutions as never before. The trichotomy begins with (1) oppression and exploitation by a ruling class, such as Wall Street and the government it buys. Next there is (2) a rebel group that struggles to capture the imagination and support of (3) the majority of the given population. If it does not, it is eventually crushed, sometimes from within by infiltrators, sometimes from without by selective or corrupt prosecution, or ultimately brutally by police-state tactics such as tear gas, rubber bullets, concussion grenades, beatings, or even police killings of protestors. If, on the other hand, the rebel group can manage to sway public opinion to their side, a revolution is possible. A worldwide revolution is imminent in 2016, although fragile and under siege. Rebellion supporting any such revolution must be nonviolent as a moral imperative as well as in recognition of the practical reality that the ownership and ruling classes have armed the local police, federal law enforcement such as Homeland Security, and National Guard to alarming levels, employing an array of lethal and non-lethal weapons, often with impunity.

The Second Renaissance will require a revolution, hopefully bloodless, to create a real democracy that has never actually existed except in such glimmering experiments as the current Occupy movement and their historical predecessors down through the ages back, at least, to the works of historical Jesus.

The Second Dark Ages looms large with the plagues on humanity in the form of corporate-fascism, militarism, and state-terrorism—including United States' drones, secret prisons, and arms sales to war zones all over the globe. The machinations of dark and unaccountable entities such as the CIA and NSA will worsen in the Second Dark Ages, building on a long history of false flag operations as evidenced by their recent counterfeiting of United States dollars and blaming the scheme on North Korea just as Bush cronies had cited the tons of chemical weapons sold to Iraq by Donald Rumsfeld, when he was an arms dealer, as evidence that Iraq still possessed weapons of mass destruction, all the while knowing that Iraq had actually cooperatively destroyed the chemicals and their long range rockets after the first Gulf War.

The Second Renaissance may begin with electoral politics in 2016, civil disobedience, and alternate media, but it will require a much more aggressive, pervasive, and relentless pursuit. General strikes may be required to starve the beast and nullify the greed that feeds it.

The Second Dark Ages is currently in negotiations by virtue of the austerity measures currently aggravating the world recession, from Argentina to Greece to Italy to each of the fifty United States, into what soon will become a world depression—the magnitude of which will likely destroy even the much vaunted BRICS economies of Brazil, Russia, India, China, and South Africa. If the "solutions" to the depression are the same as those anti-stimulus plans that have caused the recession and will cause the depression, then collapse is inevitable and imminent.

The Second Renaissance will require a truce on the culture wars, border squabbles, and trade conflicts. More importantly, we will need to regulate corporations—as chartered entities, not persons—especially financial and transnational corporations. We will also need to end the race-to-the-bottom phenomena of tax-haven shopping and sweat-labor shopping where wealthy transnational corporations produce goods in the least expensive but most exploitive labor markets and then hide the profits in offshore accounts in countries, such as the

Cayman Islands, which serve as little more than states of money laundering.

The Second Dark Ages will protect these same corporations and even fortify them, eventually either relinquishing every possible government asset and service or selling them off to the profiteers who will extract their tons of flesh by exploiting resources, lowering wages, reducing expensive safety programs, and offering inferior services with little or no accountability in a regulatory scheme that will likely become only nominal or also privatized so that industries will regulate—or not—themselves on the "honor system" as George W. Bush called it.

The Second Renaissance will require all peoples to enforce their constitutions to the fullest and in the interest of the many, not the few, as Bolivian President Evo Morales did recently when he expelled the Drug Enforcement Agency of the United States from his country as a matter of "dignity and sovereignty" of the Bolivian people. "They repressed in Bolivia. That has ended," Morales announced, adding, "For the first time since Bolivia was founded, the United States will now respect Bolivia's rules and laws." Some few constitutions may need some amending, but most current constitutions are theoretically democratic. We must turn the theory into practice. This will require abolition of monetarism of the national economies in which private entities, such as our Federal Reserve Bank, profit, by margin, off each dollar in circulation, which they control secretively and almost entirely unaccountably. We will need to recalculate usury laws to bring them back well below 10 percent from the current rates of 18 to 36 percent or even higher with the myriad fees of predatory payday lenders.

The Second Dark Ages will rely on the expertise of such technocrats as the two recently appointed prime ministers in Italy and Greece, each and both tasked to dismantle social services, reduce regulations, and—most of all—privatize. The ownership class lost untold trillions in the speculative bubble they engineered in the mortgage and derivative markets, so they now look to privatize every possible function of government from which they might derive profit, starting with pensions. Social Security is solvent and flush. Wall Street wants a cut. The ownership class has directed the ruling class that serves them to deliver the middle class and all of their social services, especially Social Security and Medicare.

The Second Renaissance will destroy the ownership and ruling classes' corrupt and self-serving grip on the levers of power so that the middle and working classes can govern in a manner that serves the greater good. This will cost the ownership and ruling classes only a minor portion of their income and wealth but most of their uspurped power.

The Second Dark Ages will destroy the long beleaguered middle class, working class, and poor at little or no cost to the ownership and ruling classes—indeed many of the already obscenely wealthy will continue to profit from the destruction.

The Second Renaissance begins with a dismantling of the American war machine by demanding that all military and war funding, by constitutional amendment, must be approved by direct supermajority of the American voters, not a congress that is completely bought by what President Eisenhower referred to as the industrial military complex.[1]

David Koch's progress: 458 percent gain in income of top 0.1 percent of Americans since the Reagan Revolution:

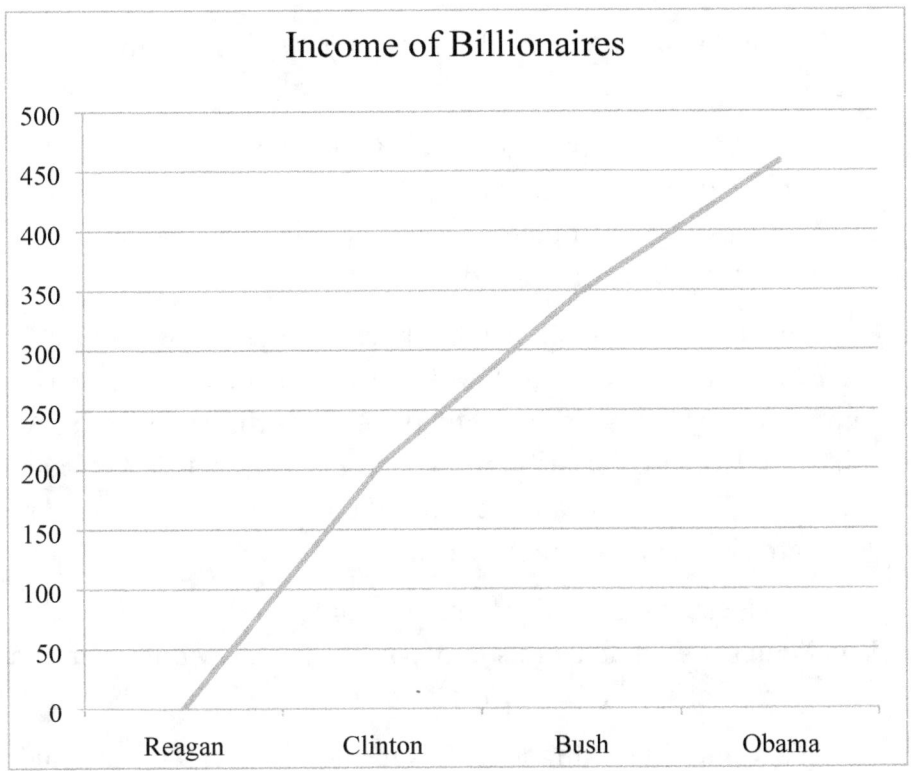

Income of Billionaires

Source: Congressional Budget Office

---

[1] Early drafts of this speech, more pointedly, referred to the military, *intelligence*, and industrial complex.

Policarpa and the Sons of America

Policarpa Salavarrieta was raised by her sister after her mother and father perished during a small pox epidemic when "La Pola" was only eleven.

Simón Bolívar was raised, largely, by his slave nanny, Hipólita.

Colombia commemorates Both Bolivar and Salavarrieta on coins and currency still circulating today. Theirs was a fascinating story of nineteenth-century class war that still reverberates all over the continent today.

Much of Bolívar's family wealth from his mother's family, the Palacioses, came from slave labor in the Cocorote copper mines. Some slaves also worked the estates that Bolívar inherited from his father's family, and Bolívar, ironically, spent much of this family wealth generated partly from slave labor to "liberate" Venezuela from Spanish colonialism.

The last survivor of the original Spanish Conquistadores, Don Mancio Serra de Leguisamo, wrote the below observations of the original sons of Americans, the Incans:

> We found these kingdoms in such good order, and the said Incas governed them in such wise [manner] that throughout them there was not a thief, nor a vicious man, nor an adulteress, nor was a bad woman admitted among them, nor were there immoral people. The men had honest and useful occupations. The lands, forests, mines, pastures, houses and all kinds of products were regulated and distributed in such sort that each one knew his property without any other person seizing it or occupying

it, nor were there law suits respecting it... the motive which obliges me to make this statement is the discharge of my conscience, as I find myself guilty. For we have destroyed by our evil example, the people who had such a government as was enjoyed by these natives. They were so free from the committal of crimes or excesses, as well men as women, that the Indian who had 100,000 pesos worth of gold or silver in his house, left it open merely placing a small stick against the door, as a sign that its master was out. With that, according to their custom, no one could enter or take anything that was there. When they saw that we put locks and keys on our doors, they supposed that it was from fear of them, that they might not kill us, but not because they believed that anyone would steal the property of another. So that when they found that we had thieves among us, and men who sought to make their daughters commit sin, they despised us.[2]

Leguisamo's deathbed confession here is exaggerated at least in that the Spanish had not entirely destroyed the Incans or their self-governance. The Incans survive today, many following after the traditional farming, religion, and clothing practices of centuries of Incan culture. The point was well taken, nevertheless; the Incan people were well established, well developed, and well governed in the Americas before the Spanish arrived to conquer them.

At his father's former military academy *Milicias de Veraguas,* Bolívar first donned a uniform and studied weaponry, strategy, and military history. In Paris after graduation, Bolívar attended the coronation of Napoleon

---

[2] Sir Clements Markham, *The Incas of Peru*, 2nd ed. London: John Murray, 1912, 300.

Bonaparte at Notre Dame. The majesty of the spectacle enchanted the young Bolívar, who returned to Venezuela to attain similar acclaim. To that end, Bolívar drafted his *Cartagena Manifesto* in what is now Colombia, and by 1813 Bolívar gained command of a Congress of United Provinces of New Granada military unit. Bolívar and his unit invaded Venezuela where he first earned his epithet, *El Libertador* in Mérida. On June 15 Bolívar read his infamous *Decree of War to the Death* and went on to capture Caracas in August and proclaim the restoration of the independent Republic of Venezuela. The decree began in bold rhetoric:

Venezuelans:

An army of brothers, sent by the Supreme Congress of New Granada, has come to liberate you, and it now stands among you, after having expelled the oppressors from the provinces of Mérida and Trujillo.

We are sent to destroy the Spaniards, to protect Americans, and to reestablish the republican governments that formed the Federation of Venezuela. The states protected by our arms are once again ruled by their former constitutions and leaders, in the full enjoyment of their freedom and independence, because our sole mission is to break the chains of servitude that still oppress some of our people, not to make laws or seize power, as the rules of war might authorize us to do.

Moved by your misfortunes, we could not witness with indifference the afflictions visited upon you by the savage Spaniards, who have annihilated and destroyed you with pillage and death, who have violated the sanctity of human rights, rendered null the most solemn articles of surrender and treaty, and committed every imaginable crime, reducing Venezuela to the most horrific desolation. Thus, justice demands retribution, and necessity obliges us to take it. Let the monsters who have infested Colombian soil, covering it with blood, vanish forever; let their punishment be equal to the enormity of their perfidy, thus washing away the stain of our ignominy and demonstrating to the nations of the world that one cannot offend the sons of America with impunity.[3]

By "sons of America," Bolívar meant the citizens of Latin America. In 1813 Spain controlled the largest empire in the world, though within Europe, it was a second-rate power, especially economically. France, the low countries, and Great Britain outperformed Spain in most any market, despite Spain's imperial policy controlling all trade between its colonies and foreign countries. The policy was, unenforced though, as it was unenforceable. Bolívar's description, however, could apply to virtually any colonial campaign before or since—including those by the United States.

Bolívar's Decree, on the other hand, remained in force until the Treaty of Santa Ana de Trujillo in November of 1820. Bolívar had marched his forces through Los Horcones, La Victoria, Valencia, and effectively re-established the Venezuelan Republic upon his triumphant August 1820 entrance into the city of Caracas, thus liberating the "Americans" from the imperial powers of Spain.

Meanwhile, another liberator, Jose San Martín of Argentina had convinced the governments of Santiago and Buenos Aires to sail a fleet on the Pacific. The project began slowly, however, due to a Spanish blockade at Valparaíso and warfare

---

[3] Frederick Fornoff, *El Libertador: Writings of Simón Bolívar*. London: Oxford University Press, 2003, 115.

in the mountains. San Martín resigned in disappointment over the delays only to have his resignation rejected and the project finally proceed. In August of 1820, the Chilean Navy set sail from Valparaiso for southern Peru with San Martín's Army in bay. After conquering Pisco on September 11 of the same year, San Martín announced the following:

> My announcement is not that of a conqueror that tries to create a new enslavement. I cannot help but be an accidental instrument of justice and agent of destiny. The outcome of victory will make Peru's capital see for the first time their sons united, freely choosing their government and emerging into the face of earth among the rank of nations.[4]

San Martín's attempts at inciting insurrection among the locals met with little action. He was loath to attack the royalists in Lima directly, as Lima was the *de facto* capital of the Spanish colonies in South America. Neither did any of San Martín's diplomatic efforts achieve independence. San Martín advanced north by sea to Huacho in November, where he first heard of Gregorio Escobedo's emancipation of port city Guayaquil, now Ecuador's largest metropolitan area with over 3 million citizens. Rebel victories by Alvarez de Arenales in Guacarillo and Pasco around the same time emboldened San Martín to promulgate *Los Reglamentos Provisionales*, design the first flag of Peru, and descend on Lima in March, which was autumn in the Southern Hemisphere.

San Martín sent one contingency to one flank and another to the other to surround Lima so that he could negotiate with

---

[4] John Lynch, *San Martin: Argentine Soldier, American Hero*. New Haven: Yale University press, 2009.

Viceroy Serna. Serna would not agree to independence, and San Martín would not accept the continuation of the Spanish Constitution of 1812, so San Martín suggested a constitutional monarchy with a Spanish head of state. The Viceroy declined two days later, after discussions with other royalists, on the grounds that Serna, as Viceroy, did not have authority to crown a monarch. In the South American winter month of July, Serna and his royalist forces abandoned Lima and retreated to the hills. San Martín and his rebel forces occupied the city, where San Martín founded the national library of Peru with a donation of his own books and the newly independent Peruvians elected him "Protector" of their new nation.

San Martín then met with Bolívar in Guayaquil to hold secret talks on the future of Latin America. San Martín was a military man at heart, not interested in ruling. Bolívar was a politician down to his very soul and entertained grand notions of establishing himself the Napoleon of the South. Although the details of the talks were not recorded, San Martín deigned to return to Argentina on a comfortable ranch, before ultimately retiring in Europe, where he lived until 1850. This left Bolívar to pursue his quest to "liberate" more Americans and expand *Gran Colombia* on the grandest possible scale. The Peruvian congress ironically named Bolívar, "the Liberator," dictator of Peru on February 10, 1824; Bolívar wasted no time in completely reorganizing the military and government to his liking before setting off for further conquests.

In royalist New Granada, Spanish General Pablo Morillo, "*El Pacificador*," vanquished the war-weary sons of America. "*El Libertador*" had led a campaign to liberate The Spanish colony of New Granada in 1819. Life in New Granada under "The

Pacifier" had been anything but peaceful for the indigenous. Morillo rounded up suspected rebels and former patriots of the first republic for indentured servitude, confiscation of land, or execution by firing squad for the more infamous rebels such as Policparpa Salavarrieta. Bodies of the executed were paraded through town as warning to others.[5]

Salavarrieta had collected and supplied much valuable information to the revolution working as a domestic under a pseudonym and forged documents in the Spanish Royalist stronghold at Bogotá. She and her brother also recruited insurgents for the cause. Salavarrieta's operation went well until Royalist guards discovered two of her compatriots, the Alymeda brothers, smuggling documents out of town. But it was not until the arrest of Alejo Sabaraín with a list of insurgent patriots, including Policarpa Salavarrieta, that the Royalists formally accused "La Pola" of treason, espionage, encouraging troops to desert, and smuggling ammunition, similar activtities of Harriet Tubman in the United States.

After a mockery of a trial, the War Council sentenced Salavarreita, her brother, and the Alymeda brothers to death by firing squad. The night before her execution, Salavarrieta vociferously cursed the Spaniards, predicted their ultimate defeat, and refused to take even a glass of water from her captors. The next day, November 14, 1817, she continued her tirade, refusing to pray with the two priests accompanying her to her demise, firmly establishing the triumph of her indomitable will in martyrdom.

------

[5]Adams, Jerome R., *Notable Latin American Women*. Jefferson, North Carolina: McFarland & Company, 1995, 75–82.

The repression and tax increases by the Royalists continued to incite rebellion. In an effort to capitalize on unrest, Bolívar entered the outlying New Granada province of Casanare, which had remained independent and anti-royalist. Bolívar appointed his loyal General Santander as governor in 1818, although Casanare was still officially a province of New Granada. After victory at the Battle of Boyacá the next year, Bolívar consolidated power over the next two years and participated in drafting the constitution of *Gran Colombia*. Soon thereafter, the new congress elected Santander as Vice President. *Presidente* Bolívar then left *Gran Colombia* to Santander's leadership and returned to Venezuela to propose uniting the two new Bolívarian republics.

Santander, a more thoughtful and able administrator than Bolívar, presided over several crises in Bolívar's absence. The years of wars left the economy strained while remnants of royalist sentiment haunted the new republic. Santander responded decisively and brutally by executing the captured Spanish officers then in jail. Bolívar wrote to express his regret and disapproval, but this was not an act that he could undo, though he did rescind some of Santander's other official acts. The new vice president also reduced or eliminated many of the tariffs and taxes of the Spanish and opened all ports to foreign trade.

Bolívar returned from military campaigns in 1826 to internal division and dissent, which included regional uprisings in Venezuala. Bolívar declared a general amnesty in an attempt to preserve the union, but this act did not sit well across the border in the former New Granada, so Bolívar proposed a new constitution to re-unite the disintegrating confederation.

During the April 1828 convention at Ocaña, Bolívar proposed a stronger central government with a president for life, right of the president to name a successor, and a hereditary third chamber of the legislature. Santander and other more liberal minds formed a faction in opposition to Bolívar's Napoleonic notions. The two factions negotiated for months, ultimately drafting a document which was so liberal as to cause Bolívar and his followers to walk out, thereby precluding a super-majority necessary to ratify the document.

Among Bolívar's guiding texts while composing his constitution were Voltaire's *Letters*, Montesquieu's *Spirit of the Laws*, and Smith's *The Wealth of Nations*. It is difficult to know whether or not Bolívar noted the irony in any of his actions, given Bolívar's dream to create a federation of all the now independent Latin American republics with a federal government established primarily to enforce the rights of the citizen.

"El Libertador" referred to himself in letters as a "liberal," meaning he believed in a free market and freedom from colonialism. Bolívar was a student of both the French and American Revolutions; he even sent his nephew to study at the University of Virginia to be close to Thomas Jefferson, though Bolívar argued against slavery regularly, after having benefitted from it financially through inheritance. Bolívar did, however, reject the fullness of the American model of democracy as too loose for Latin America, which he opined bore a "triple yoke" of ignorance, tyranny, and vice as a legacy of Spanish colonialism. Bolívar also went as far as to blame the

fall of his first administration on idealistic subordinates who perseverated on an unrealistic notion of some foolish "ethereal" republic.[6]

On August 27, 1828, "The Liberator," hypocritically decreed himself dictator of the several newly independent republics in an attempt to unite what is now Venezuela, Ecuador, Colombia, and Bolivia. Colombia's internationally famous twentieth-century man of letters, Gabriel García Márquez, wrote a novel depicting Bolívar's final years as dictator, *The General in his Labyrinth*, which is reportedly a favorite of the current president of Venezuela, Hugo Chavez. Márquez summed up the disappointment of Bolívar's dreams in a foreshadowing comment "The Liberator" made to his aide regarding the United States, "omnipotent and terrible, and that its tale of liberty will end in a plague of miseries for us all."[7] As many revolutionary leaders have before and since, Bolívar became all too like his vanquished foes in their tyrannical attempts to govern and preserve unity.

Bolívar resigned his presidency in 1830 and planned to exile himself to France after failing to unite Latin America. He began crating his writings and other possessions but died of tuberculosis on December 17. Oddly, Bolívar requested that his aide-de-camp burn Bolívar's extensive speeches, letters, and other writings. General Daniel F. O'Leary ignored the

---

[6] David Bushnell, *Simon Bolivar: Liberation and Disappointment.* New York: Pearson Longman, 2004, 17.

[7] Gabriel Garcia Marquez, *The General in His Labyrinth.* New York: Vintage, Trans. Edith Grossman, 1990, 223.

deathbed request, fortunately, realizing their historical significance.

Indeed, the legacy of Bolívar's political and military campaigns continues to present day with the leadership of Hugo Chavez and Evo Morales each paying homage in many speeches and programs. Statues of Bolívar adorn plazas from Paris to Paraguay. The Bolívar, in fact, remains the name of the present currency of Venezuela, and Bolivia remains eponymous of its founder.

Colombia celebrates Salavarrieta today as the Grand Heroine of the Colombian Independence and portrays her likeness on the 10,000 peso note. The people of Colombia, and Bolivia, unfortunately, suffer from world drug trade and wars related to their traditional coca leaf and a sort of neo-colonialism of global "free trade," both of which current Bolivian president and former llamaherd, Evo Morales, campaigned to cease. Salavarrieta, Bolívar, San Martín, Santander, and the contemporary Morales each and all prove the trichotomy of rebellion in their ultimate ability to persuade the masses to revolt against an exploitative elite in class warfare. Unfortunately, as if often the case in twenty-first century politics, Bolívar, who enjoyed an upper class upbringing, claimed to, and often did, fight for the common class, but eventually became co-opted and or imitated the ruling class that he professed to oppose.

The One-Percenters

"Class warfare is being waged in America,

and the wrong side is winning."

—Bernie Sanders

The top one percent currently earn over $348,000 annually.

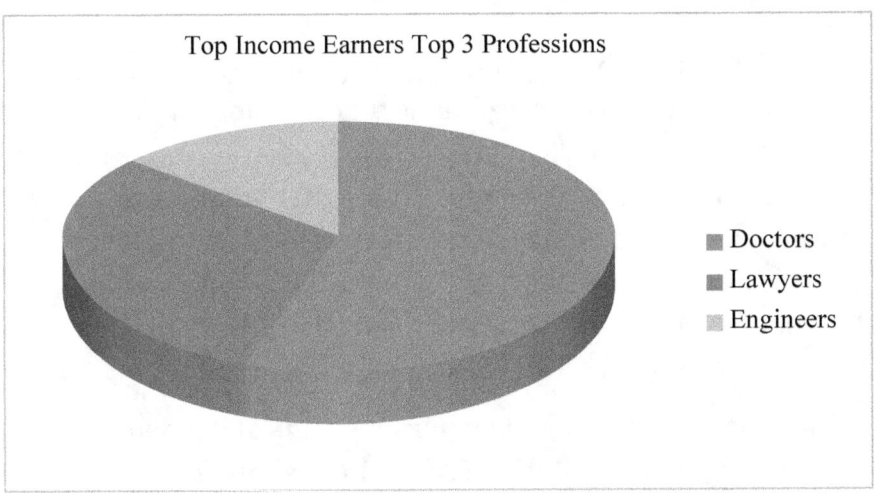

Source: Congressional Budget Office

Many of the one percent, by income as opposed to wealth, occupy the medical, legal, and engineering professions. The threshold of the top one-percent is over $348,000 annually— over twenty times poverty level income. Some of the one percenters' income is from dividends, interest, rent, and royalty payments on copyrights or patents. Wealthy individuals and families can easily earn enough off their wealth so as not to need to bother with work.

The income that American families received from dividends, interest, and rents surpassed the income that American families earned from work during the so-called Reagan Revolution. Since then, the share of gross domestic product created by the manufacturing sector fell from 21 percent to 14 percent; conversely, the share of gross domestic product created by the financial services sector rose from 14 to 21 percent during the same time.

At the turn of the last century the powers that were still worried about the labor problems that remained, if not festered, since Pennsylvania militia and federal troops fed striking 1877 railroad workers "a rifle diet for a few days," at the suggestion of Thomas Alexander Scott, president of the railroad. Then there were the bloody suppressions of the Haymarket Riot in 1886 Chicago, and the 1892 Homestead Strike at Carnegie's steel works.

Italy is currently having labor problems of its own. The recent resignation of Italian Prime Minister Silvio Berlusconi, whose personal media fortune is valued at over $5 billion was long in coming, but his fellow one-percenters became unhappy with Berlusconi.

His replacement was former academic and European Commissioner Mario Monti, a technocrat who was charged to implement austerity measures more drastic than Berlusconi could advocate, given Berlusconi's personal wealth. Monti's close relationship with European central bankers foretold the future of Italy. The immediate future in Italy, with its economy that it larger than that of India, was one of a national unity government struggling with a liquidity crisis and pressure to follow Greece in recession or depression creating economic programs in the name of budget balancing. As a practical matter, Italians faced pension theft, theft by privatization, and social program theft by globalist one-percenters. The rates on Italian debt rose the week of November 13, 2011 to over 7 percent, yet the 2012 budget lists a conservative 3 percent deficit, while the United Kingdom runs 10 percent deficit, and the United States over 30 percent. Italy's debt calculated to a troubling 120 percent of Gross Domestic Product, though not significantly higher than the 90 percent of the United States. Monti wasted no time in reporting to the European Commission in Brussels that his fledgling administration would honor all promises of his government to institute harsh, anti-union and anti-working class austerity measures. Two prime ministers later, Matteo Renzi earned his "troublemaker" moniker with *The Economist* in January 2016 by declaring an end to days of the European Union dictating economic policy of Italy by "remote control" from Brussels.

Greece, apparently by remote control, installed former European Central Bank Vice President Lucas Papademos as the prime minister after behind-the-scenes machinations scuttled the promised referendum on the $177 billion bailout package. It is not coincidental that Papademos helped Greece make the original transition from the drachma to the euro. Many placed hope in Greece's progressive and visionary finance minister, Yanis Varoufakis, but Brussels pressed the mute button on him in summer 2015, forcing him to resign to make way for more bailouts for mostly German banks that made irresponsible investments that preyed on Greek small businesses and pensioners.

It is not a coincidence that many of the same one-percenters who have steadily reduced their tax burden over the last few decades are the same one-percenters who hold and profit from much of the debt of the sinking middle class and struggling lower class. They are also the same one-percenters who will not hear of returning their tax rates to Clinton or Reagan era levels. They have their minioins in congress to assure the debate rarely wanders from the "spending problem" narrative of the anti-government types, who often make good use of the social programs they mock while cheating on their taxes or failing to pay child support.

Tea Party hypocrite Representative Chip Cravaack of Minnesota recently ran on an anti-government platform at the same time that he cashed government disability payments totaling $92,273 for the sleep apnea that he claimed ended his pilot career for Northwest Airlines. Fellow conservative Republican Representative John Fleming of Louisiana, meanwhile, complained that he simply could not afford the tax increase for the wealthy that President Obama suggested. Fleming went on to explain that, as a small businessman, he had "maybe $400,000 left over" after feeding his family.

Representative Joe Walsh of Illinois, who currently owes $117,000 in child support, recently interrupted a constituent complaining about the banks with this diatribe:

> That's not the problem! The problem is you've got to be consistent. And I don't want government meddling in the marketplace. Yeah, they move from Goldman Sachs to the

White House, I understand all of that. But you gotta' be consistent. And it's not the private marketplace that created this mess. What created mess was your government, which has demanded for years that everybody be in a home. And we've made it easy as possible for people to be in homes. Don't blame banks, and don't blame the marketplace for the mess we're in right now! I am tired of hearing that crap! This pisses me off! Too many people don't listen.

It should disgust, although not surprise, us all to know that Representative Walsh received over $200,000 in campaign contributions in 2012 from securities and investment, insurance, business services, lawyer, lobbyist, and commercial banking interests. This is for an incumbent in a safe district. Of further interest is that Walsh found $35,000 to lend his own campaign; not a penny for his own children from his first wife, though. Walsh is as greedy, selfish, and immoral as his corporate contributors. What is worse is the Christian image Walsh cultivates, winning endorsement from Tony Perkins and the Family Research Council:

> We thank Congressman Walsh who has voted consistently to defend faith, family and freedom. Congressman Walsh and other 'True Blue Members' have voted to repeal Obamacare, de-fund Planned Parenthood, end government funding for abortion within the health care law, uphold the Defense of Marriage Act, and continue support for school choice. I applaud their commitment to uphold the institutions of marriage and family.

Jesus would not approve.

If he were alive today, Yeshua, or Jesus, might be labeled a liberal, a socialist, or a class warrior for his words and deeds. Jesus condemned the greedy money changers and forgave prostitutes. He fed the masses; he opposed capital punishment, though he cruelly and ironically died by it.

As few after him would, historical Jesus challenged all forms of tyranny and corruption, whether it be the tyranny of the Romans, or the corruption of the Jewish Aristocrats, or even the common hypocrites. His ways were always non-violent, which would inspire Jesus' later followers Mahatmas Gandhi and Martin Luther King. Just as Gandhi and King were assassinated for inciting class war rebellion, so too was Jesus. They were no one-percenters, for "It is easier for a camel to go through the eye of a needle, than for a rich man to enter into the kingdom of God." (Matthew: 19; 23)

The topic of class war has been taboo for decades in the United States, associated with communism and overthrow of the government. America must actively reject this, however, and discuss class war politics and economics with family, neighbors, co-workers and engage in electoral politics—as a beginning not an end. Progressives should remind all who will listen that the United States is a constitutional republic that grants only those powers to the government that are listed in the constitution itself, one of which is the power—and the duty—to "provide for the general welfare" of the citizenry. This social contract theory traces back to Thomas Hobbes calling for government to ensure safety and well-being, as also expressed in the "general good" concept of the 1620 Mayflower Compact:

> Having undertaken, for the Glory of God, and advancements of the Christian faith and honor of our King and Country, a voyage to plant the first colony in the Northern parts of Virginia, do by these presents, solemnly

and mutually, in the presence of God, and one another, covenant and combine ourselves together into a civil body politic; for our better ordering, and preservation and furtherance of the ends aforesaid; and by virtue hereof to enact, constitute, and frame, such just and equal laws, ordinances, acts, constitutions, and offices, from time to time, as shall be thought most meet and convenient for the general good of the colony; unto which we promise all due submission and obedience.

Indeed, humans are social animals, and the family—the smallest social unit, and one that conservatives claim to revere—regularly "covenant and combine" together for mutual betterment.

So Many Tigers

Geronimo dedicated his autobiography to Theodore Roosevelt.

First a shaman, Geronimo was only eventually elected a chief after a fierce battle which took the life of Geronimo's predecessor. No army ever captured the shaman or chief, and although Geronimo surrendered several times and died in captivity on a reservation at the age of 80, he never surrendered unconditionally. Britton Davis, one of several United States cavalry leaders to pursue Geronimo described him as "a thoroughly vicious, intractable, and treacherous man." With no apparent hint of irony, Lieutenant Davis went on to complain that Geronimo's "word, no matter how earnestly pledged, was worthless."[8]

Geronimo was always a warrior. He fought for a class that is now amongst the poorest of the poor in America: natives relegated to reservations.

For his part, Geronimo could have pointed to numerous betrayals by several United States generals acting on behalf of several successive presidents. The "greatest of wrongs," according to Geronimo, perpetrated against Geronimo's Bedonkohe Apache occured in 1863 when General West lured then Chief Mangas Coloradas (red sleeves) to New Mexico with promises of kind treatment only to assassinate the leader, sever his head, and send the skull to Washington to be weighed

---

[8]Britton Davis, *The Truth about Geronimo.* Lincoln: University of Nebraska Press, 1976, viii.

and displayed, where it remains today at the Smithsonian Institution.[9]

Geronimo had opposed the surrender and stayed in Arizona with a separate contingency that had, unfortunately, sent most of their weapons with the ill-fated Mangas Coloradas. Upon learning of the treachery against his trusting people, Geronimo led those Apache remaining with him back up into the mountains again. Low on supplies, his group happened upon some four white cattle herders, so Geronimo and his band killed all four of them to take the cattle for meat. Mitigating the murder was the lack of scalping—due to the fact that the whites were ranchers, not warriors. While still butchering the cattle, Geronimo and his Apache fell victim to an attack of United States troops who surprised the band so effectively as to kill seven. The troops heavily out-armed the Apache, with spears, bows, and arrows. The Apache scattered, intending to regroup at their pre-determined rendezvous some fifty miles away. The cavalry would attack Geronimo two more times along the way before returning to their camp.

The first year of Geronimo's tenure was peaceful, but the following winter brought a new attack by the cavalry, killing seven children, five women, and four warriors. The troops confiscated all of the food, blankets, clothes, and horses. Then they destroyed the tepees. Geronimo and his few remaining tribe members had nothing left and experienced their coldest winter ever. Geronimo took three warriors and trailed the troops back to the reservation at San Carlos. After assuring the cavalry that they would stay in camp, Geronimo and his three

---

[9]S.M.Barrett, *Geronimo: His Own Story.* New York: Meridian, 1996, 121.

warriors encountered an American and Mexican on horseback. The Apaches shot the two off their horses and rode them back to take their sick to Hot Springs, where Chief Victorio and the Warm Springs Apaches hosted Geronimo's band for over a year in perfect peace.

Geronimo's first encounter with whites was also peaceful. Soon after the "Kas-ki-yeh Massacre" of 1858, Geronimo had met a group of civilian land surveyors who readily greeted the Apaches. The whites and the Apaches camped near each other and traded buckskin, blankets, and ponies for shirts, provisions, and coins. The first Europeans to encounter Apaches were from Coronado's Spanish expedition of 1541; the explorer wrote of them:

> After seventeen days of travel, I came upon a rancheria of the Indians who follow these cattle (bison). These natives are called Querechos. They do not cultivate the land, but eat raw meat and drink the blood of the cattle they kill. They dress in the skins of the cattle (bison), with which all the people in this land clothe themselves, and they have very well-constructed tents (teepees), made with tanned and greased cowhides, in which they live and which they take along as they follow the cattle. They have dogs which they load to carry their tents, poles, and belongings.[10]

Apache plains dogs were somewhat smaller than those used for pulling loads by Canadian peoples. The Apache dogs were beasts of burden that pulled loads up to fifty pounds as much as twenty miles a day. The Apache and Apachean people

---

[10] Hammond, George P., & Rey, Agapito (Eds.), *Narratives of the Coronado Expedition 1540-1542.* Albuquerque: University of New Mexico Press, 1940.

entered the plains from the north as early as 1300 and eventually continued migrating into what are now Texas, New Mexico, Arizona, and northern Mexico, where they encountered Euro-American settlers in the 1800s.

While on the Plains, the Apache traded their hunted bison meat, hides, and stones for tools with the Pueblo Indians for their maize and woven cotton goods. The Apache wintered near the Pueblos in well-established camps in complete peace until Spanish rule disrupted the trade by subjugating the Pueblos to mission work. The Apache acquired horses, horsemanship, and left the area, fleeing Spanish domination. The Spaniards and Apache had a long and checkered history of trading with each other in one village one year and raiding each other elsewhere the next year. This uneasy tradition continued after Mexico won its independence and white settlers moved into the southwest to ranch. By 1835 the Mexican government placed a high bounty on Apache scalps, and two years later Chief Compas of the Mimbreño Apaches earned a hunter a sizable bounty for the delivery of the Chief's scalp to the federal authorities. Mangas Coloradas (Red Sleeves) rose to replace Compas as chief and led a series of raid against Mexican forces to avenge the fallen chief.

So strained were relations for so long that over a decade later many Apache bands promised safe passage to U.S. troops during the Mexican-American War. Chief Mangas Coloradas went as far as inviting United States General Stephen Watts Kearny to join forces with the Apache in conquering northern Mexico. This unwritten treaty eased the effort of invading and conquering what is now Texas. Mangas Coloradas signed a peace treaty with the Americans after the war, but this peace was short-lived, due to an immigration of gold miners into the Santa Rita Mountains in the late 1850s, and so began what came to be known as "The Apache Wars."

Although the Apache culture was perhaps more bellicose and independent than some tribes, other factors such as geography played a role in extending the "Indian problem" with the Apache after most other tribes had long been "pacified." As the United States is re-learning in Afghanistan, mountain warfare is treacherous and lends great advantages to smaller, more nimble forces, especially when the forces are defending homeland that they know better than their invading adversaries. Geronimo and his fellow tribesmen used their mountaineering skills much to their advantage during decades of battle. Each side raided the other's horses, supplies, and weapons whenever the opportunity presented. Each side killed innocent civilians, including women and children, and each side suffered high casualties. The stereotype of the Apache as the most savage of the native-American Indians is, however, unwarranted. The motives of the Apache were simple and clear: to live in peace on ancestral lands in their traditional culture. The whites, to the Apaches' mind, were duplicitous and violent invaders who desecrated the land with mines and fences.

Geronimo told the story of losing his aged mother, his young wife, and his three small children in Kas-ki-yeh during a raid by Mexican soldiers after Geronimo had taken several of his Bedonkohe Apache to the Sonoran town of Casa Grande to trade. Then Chief Mangas Coloradas decided that, with only 80 warriors and no weapons, the Bedonkohe should retreat to their home in Arizona, leaving the fallen dead on the earth.

Geronimo recalled in his biography that he did not pray or resolve to do "anything in particular," for he had "no purpose left," so he "followed the tribe silently," staying barely within earshot of his band of Apache.[11] Upon return to Arizona, Geronimo burned his mother's and his family's teepees, along with his children's playthings. Soon thereafter, Chief Mangas Coloradas called a council, where the warriors resolved to take the warpath to Mexico to avenge their kinsman. Geronimo's Bedonkohe then went to meet with the Chokonen Apache warriors and their chief, Cochise. Geronimo spoke to urge these warriors to follow him into battle; he admonished them not to mourn for him should he die in battle over the border, for, if he were to fall, he would fall in the country where his family had fallen. The Bedonkohe and the Chokonen set out Southwest to enlist the warriors of the Nedni Apaches and their chief, Whoa.

In the summer of 1859, then, the three Apache bands painted their faces, banded their foreheads with buckskin, and marched thirty to fifty miles per day into Mexico to avenge their fallen kinsman. On the first night of skirmishes, the Apache captured a supply wagon with provisions and more rifles. The next day brought out two companies of Mexican infantry and two more companies of cavalry. Geronimo's Apache contingency engaged them with guerilla tactics, rifles, bows, arrows, spears, commandeered sabers of fallen Mexicans, and knives until only Geronimo and three other Apaches stood on the field over dozens of vanquished opponents. The last of the fighting ended when two Mexican

---

[11]S.M.Barrett, *Geronimo: His Own Story.* New York: Meridian, 1996, 77.

reinforcements shot two of the remaining Apache only to be slain themselves by Geronimo: one with a saber, and the final by Geronimo's knife. Upon rendezvous with the other two Apache bands, the braves surrounded Geronimo and elected him the new war chief of all three bands. Geronimo rejoiced in his avenge of his family at the massacre of "Kas-ki-yeh."

By the time the Americans had come to have an "Indian Problem," the Apache had experienced many problems with the Spanish and Mexican settlement on Apache ancestral land. The Treaty of Guadalupe-Hidalgo established in 1848 that the United States were, thenceforth, responsible for the Apache "problem" on either side of the border. The first recorded bloodshed occurred in 1837 by an American trader by the name of John "James" Johnson, who invited Apache to trade with his mining party in New Mexico. Johnson ambushed the would-be trading partners with rifles and a cannon loaded with glass, chain, and iron scraps. Chief Juan José Compá and 20 of his Chilhene Apache band died in the massacre. Fourteen years later Chief Mangas Coloradas suffered the torture and humiliation of miners tying him to a tree to whip him in front of his band after the Chief had urged the miners to seek their fortunes elsewhere. Chief Cochise, ten years later, lost several relatives at the hands of the United States Army in the "Bascom Affair." In 1872, however, Cochise negotiated peace with General Oliver Howard and retired on a reservation near Fort Bowie, where Cochise died of natural causes.

Indian Commissioner L.E. Dudley and the United States Army removed over 1400 Yavapai and Dilzhe'e Apache from thousands of acres of lands set aside on Rio Verde Indian Reserve in 1875. Several hundred perished in the 180-mile winter march to San Carlos, where they were interned for a quarter century to protect white settlers who were busy occupying the former Apache lands. Geronimo's band of Bedonkohe Apache, however, remained free for more than ten years.

At negotiations in the field for re-surrender of Geronimo, United States Cavalry General George Crook famously reported to General Sheridan in March of 1886:

> I met the hostiles yesterday at Lieutenant Maus's camp, they being located 500 yards distant. I found them very independent, and as fierce as so many tigers; knowing what pitiless brutes they are themselves they mistrust every one else. After my talk with them it seemed as if it would be impossible to get any hold on them except on condition that they be allowed to return to the reservation on their old status.[12]

General Sheridan is credited with the infamous: "The only good Indians I ever saw were dead," but he denied authorship till his death. Geronimo is recorded by translators as protesting to General Crook that same day:

> I was living quietly and contented, doing and thinking of no harm, while at Sierra Blanca. I don't know what harm I did to those three men, Chato, Mickey Free, and Lieutenant Davis. I was living peaceably and satisfied when people began to speak bad of me. I should be glad to know who started those stories. I was living peaceably with my family, having plenty to eat, sleeping well, taking care of my people, and perfectly contented. I don't know where those bad stories first came from. There we were doing well and my people well. I was behaving well. I hadn't

[12] Britton Davis, *The Truth About Geronimo*. 198.

killed a horse or man, American or Indian. I don't know what was the matter with the people in charge of us. They knew this to be so, and yet they said I was a bad man and the worst man there: but what harm had I done? I was living peaceably and well, but I did not leave on my own accord. Had I so left it would have been right to blame me: but as it is, blame those men who started this talk about me. Some time before I left an Indian named Wodiskay had a talk with me. He said, "they are going to arrest you," but I paid no attention to him, knowing that I had done no wrong: and the wife of Mangas, "Huera," told me that they were going to seize me and put me and Mangas in the guard-house, and I learned from the American and Apache soldiers, from Chato, and Mickey Free, that the Americans were going to arrest me and hang me, and so I left.[13]

The night after General Crook completed negotiations with Geronimo and his renegade band, an American by the name of Tribolet sold the highly intoxicating mescal to both Crook's scouts and Geronimo's renegades. Geronimo and his band escaped in the night and fled to Mexico. General Crook resigned the next day.

Less than a fortnight passed before General Nelson A. Miles assumed the command. His strategy was much more thorough and grand than Crook's. Miles dismissed the Apache scouts, garrisoned all water holes and ranches, established thirty signal points on mountain tops, and set out with 5,000 troops to capture Geronimo and his remnant renegades.

Geronimo, Nachite (son of Cochise), and fewer than twenty other men, along with about the same number of women and

[13]Britton Davis, *The Truth About Geronimo.* 200-201.

children, headed south to northwestern Chihuahua outside a small town named Casas Grandes. A small diplomatic envoy of three Apache met a fateful end in town by Mexicans who had come to find more reason to side with the pursuing United States Army than the waning Apache.

General Miles' first contingent sent to pursue the renegades included a detachment of cavalry, who dismounted their beleaguered horses after 5 days in the rugged Sonoran mountains and continued on foot. The governments of Mexico and the United States had agreed that either country's militaries could cross the border in "hot pursuit" of Apache, so as to pre-empt any attempts by the renegades to use the border as a safe haven. The plan was to demoralize and harass the Apache until they were too tired to resist. Finally, on September 4, 1886 Geronimo's Bedonkohe Apache surrendered at Skeleton Creek in Arizona.

Consistent with the trichotomy of rebellion, Geronimo led his band of Apache on a long struggle against the Mexican military and the United States Cavalry. A small group of oligarchs manipulated the Mexican government to the south and corporatists dominated the American government to the north. The Apache were eventually squeezed off their ancestral lands from both ends. Geronimo perennially convinced a critical mass of his tribesmen to continue on for decades in violent war that ended with many dead on both sides. The elite oligarchs employed the usual tactics of dividing to conquer, bribing and co-opting would-be opponents, and threats of violence as well as outright violence to meet their ends.

In the end, the remaining Apache were forced onto reservations in Arizona, Oklahoma, and Florida. Geronimo's band were, however, treated with much respect by their captors for their history of fierce struggle. The United States Congress voted in 1912 to free the Apache from their internment and offered them the opportunity to move to the Mescalero Reservation in New Mexico. Nearly two-hundred did so, while fewer than one-hundred remained in Oklahoma at Fort Sill.

Though many Apache have cross-bred and assimilated, it is ironic that so many years later, even a conservative war-hawk Republican such as John McCain never fails to at least pay a visit to the Apache and Navajo on the reservations in his state while campaigning for re-election every six years. In perhaps even greater irony, Apache in both Arizona and Oklahoma currently operate successful casinos that take money from mostly white visitors in games of chance that are always designed to benefit the house—in this case the Apache house.

Death of the Middle Class

"Far and away the best prize that life offers is the chance to work hard at work worth doing"

—Theodore Roosevelt

26-year growth in income of top 1 percent of income earners as compared to that of the bottom twenty percent and the middle class in between.

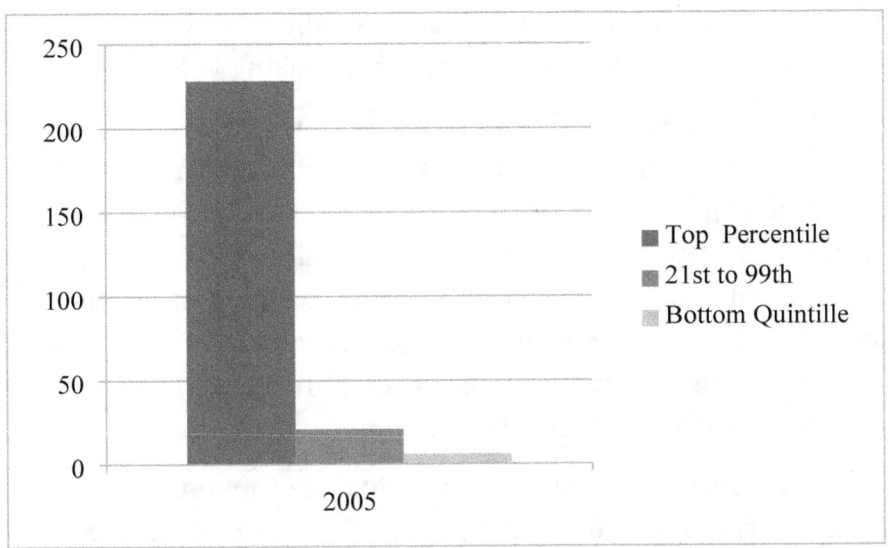

Source: Congressional Budget Office

Above the one percenters, the point-one-percenters' average $5.6 billion annual income has risen 385 percent since the Reagan Revolution. The rising tide, however, did not lift the boats of the working class—whose incomes have actually fallen over the same period of time. In the last seven years alone the median household income has fallen over 7 percent. And, a staggering forty-six million Americans, mostly children and their single mothers, live below the poverty line of $22,000 for a family of four. Nearly half of these poor live on half or less than half of the poverty line income. This calculates to one in five American children living in poverty. This is not to mention the staggering number of Americans who have, even after the passage of "Obamacare," no health insurance or the nearly one-quarter of Americans who are unemployed or underemployed, some of whom are not even officially counted by the government since they are not actively seeking work.

Neither Democrats nor Republicans even discuss poverty. The last presidential candidate who dared to broach the subject, John Edwards, was destroyed by a sex scandal. Welfare has been "reformed" into something that maintains those eligible in poverty and rejects far more for such things as drug use. The rich and super rich, on the other hand, are not stripped of their income or assets when they use illegal drugs or abuse prescription drugs.

The mention of raising the marginal tax rate on millionaires, billionaires, and corporations from the current 35 percent closer to the 70 percent rate under Nixon or the 92 percent under Eisenhower has the ruling class and their lackeys crying "class war."

So be it.

Class war it is, then.

Actually, the class war has been waged as long as the country has existed, and before it was founded. The classes change membership periodically, but there are always those at the top seeking unfair advantage in order to enrich themselves at the expense of others. Whether it's gender, race, slavery, indentured servitude, lack of women's suffrage, family lineage, immigration status, education pedigree, or felony status, there will always be demagogues manipulating groups against each other to create opportunities for the demagogues to gain privilege, power, and profit.

The American Dream, such as it ever was, is fading for most. The vast majority of Americans feel that their financial security and upward mobility are not increasing, but decreasing. This is, of course, a natural reaction to unemployment, foreclosures, and inflation of food and necessitites prices. This is to say nothing of health care costs, which have consistently outpaced inflation for decades. Nearly half of all foreclosures, in fact, are related to financial difficulties related to unexpected and uninsured health care costs.

In place of rising or even stable wages, the ruling class has placated the middle class and working class with easy and cheap credit, eventually so irresponsibly given so that many in the financial industry began to refer to such credit as "liar's loans."

Though there is no consensus as to what constitutes the middle class or working class, this book will arbitrarily assign the middle class to any person or family with income between half the median income and four times that. In 2011, that would include families with income between $25,000 and

$200,000. This leaves a gap between the official poverty line, which is inappropriately low, and the bottom of the middle class. The poverty line should rise to the level of half the median income. Any family attempting to live on $25,000 per year would likely feel more poor than middle class, especially if at least one parent is working, which brings additional expenses of commuting and work clothing or meals away from home. The working class and the middle class overlap in many definitions, and this book will define the working class as those middle class families whose income derives mostly from wages, as opposed to rents, dividends, or royalties.

President Obama's 2012 announced ten-year budget purports to address the issue of income disparity, but most agree that it would not go far enough, even if it were to pass congress intact, which is unlikely. Obama named Vice President Biden to head the new White House Task Force on the Middle Class. There is no such Task Force for the working poor. Yet, Obama's 2016 multi-year plan for "useable" nuclear weapons manages to find one trillion tax dollars.

The middle class is more than an economic issue, however. The middle class has become the most stabilizing phenomenon in the American experiment. It is well established that home ownership, long-term employment, and constancy in residency lower crime and stress rates, improve health, increase graduation rates for family members, and improves financial status in general. The decline of the middle class, conversely, is likely to worsen quality of life and political stability for an entire community or nation. While there we have seen modest gains in health and education between the middle class and the ruling class, the poor perform poorly in such measures as high school graduation, constancy in residency, teen pregnancy, and well as physical and mental health. Much of the high tech industry, government, education, military, and health sectors rely on middle class families to raise children through high school and at least some college in order to maintain quality institutions through employment.

The trends are clear. Although most baby-boomers did better than their parents, children of the boomers may or may not do as well, but the next generation is likely to see a vanishing middle class and greater difficulty financing such things as college, transportation, housing, health care, retirement, or vacation. According to Federal Reserve data, median household net worth rose 18 percent between 2004 and 2007 but the crash of 2008 destroyed it all and then some, reducing median net worth by over 3 percent between 2004 and 2008.

What is much more troubling for many families is the shift away from employment with benefits such as retirement and health insurance to independent contracts and the "gig" economy of Uber and Task Rabbit. Given the astronomical cost of major medical treatments such as most cancer procedures or most any surgery, an uninsured middle class family that unexpectedly amasses a $100,000 plus medical bill can go quickly from comfort and stability to bankruptcy with one ailment. Given the strictness of the new bankruptcy processes, a family would be stuck with the bill forever.

Perhaps of most concern to society and coming generations is the comparison to the Dark Ages and the lack of a middle class. Science, education, health care, and innovation all declined or stagnated during the Dark Ages, while slavery, serfdom, tyranny, and war all flourished. We see increases in the latter around the globe in a trend that is likely to continue. The so-called safety net is disappearing with the middle class and often causing families to go from middle class to poverty or crushing debt servitude.

It is difficult to say what would have happened if not for most families becoming double-income. Moreover, it is difficult to quantify the value of the loss of the stay at home parent. To be sure, some of the second paycheck tpyically goes to child care, commuting, work clothes, and more expensive meals.

From 1979 to 2005 after-tax income for the top 1% rose 228 percent, only 21 percent for the middle class, and a mere 6 percent for the poorest quintile, according to Congressional Budget Office statistics. These statistics are best understood graphically, as in the table at the beginning of this book.

While the economy did grow well over the period, the vast majority of the growth went to corporate and dividend profits, as opposed to wage increases or social programs. Some of the disparity is due to globalization and the unfair and unfree so-called free trade and so-called liberalization policies. Some of the disparity is due to technology making some jobs obsolete, but all of it is largely at the control of the ruling class, and since it is very much to their advantage, they did much to aggravate the situation and little or nothing to ameliorate it, mostly for selfish motives, but also as part of a sort of Ayn Rand perspective or morality, if there is any morality to it at all; perhaps it would be better to refer to it as immorality. Indeed there is a prosperity gospel movement in America, but even within it, and all major religious, greed is a vice and charity a virtue. Similarly, usury is explicitly immoral in Islam, Christianity, Buddhism, and Judaism.

Many economists and politicians rationalize the class differences as due to the business cycle or global competition, but these are phenomena that are not at the control of the middle or working classes, but largely manipulated by the ruling class. For instance, there is no reason that we cannot have both innovation and job security by means of job training programs. There is no reason that we cannot continue the Social Security system or expand Medicare to all Americans. There is no reason that we cannot regulate and tax banks, insurance, manufacturing, or any other sector more or better. There is no reason that the ruling class cannot pay more taxes so that the middle and working classes can benefit more and pay less. These are all choices—choices that have been made, thus far, in an undeclared class war of the superrich on the rest of the population.

It is not an accident that the rich and super rich are doing better than ever while the middle class wanes. This is by design. It is systemic.

AT&T donated over $462,739 to Rick Perry between 2000 and 2010, according to the Texas Ethics Commission. It is doubtful that the corporation agreed with much of Perry's opinions that climate science is a "contrived phony mess," or that "Intelligent Design should be taught in schools," or that Social Security is "Ponzi scheme," or that abortion should be illegal, or that federal income tax should be abolished; these are statements likely intended to rile Perry's ultra-conservative base. AT&T, of course, had other issues of access, monopoly, and freedom from regulation in mind when backing corporatist candidates like Perry. AT&T, like all lobbying corporations expect a return on their campaign contribution investments. Thanks to the recent Citizen's United case the Supreme Court has removed almost all restrictions of money as speech by corporations based on the notion that the corporation is a person under the Constitution, and Perry celebrated the pro-business and anti-democracy ruling—and AT&T would not have it any other way.

The most important difference between corporations and real persons, however, is that most persons survive on between $50,000 and $750 per year while corporations' annual budgets typically range from the millions to the billions. The class divide could hardly be starker. It is a wonder that the legislature conducts any business whatever on behalf of the working class in such a pay to play system. Over the decades, especially since the Reagan Revolution, the ownership class of corporations and billionaires has succeeded in reducing their share of federal income tax contributions from nearly half to less than a fifth. This is while executive pay has skyrocketed from twelve times that of the average worker to hundreds of times. In one of the most outrageous examples of both trends in a single company, International Paper Company recently raised its CEO's pay $12.3 million in the same year it paid no federal income tax whatever, instead receiving a refund of $249 million, while paying most of its workers much less than middle class wages.

And, the middle class paid the bill.

The middle class was built largely by union workers during and after World War II. So, it is more important than ever to support unions and work-place regulation, including—

primarily—collective bargaining rights. We should not cross picket lines, but rather boycott businesses that mistreat workers. American workers should establish unions where they work place if it is not union protected currently. If it is, workers should read their contract, attend their union meetings, and vigourously enforce all provisions of their collective bargaining agreements.

Bread or the Club

Emiliano loved the ladies. The ladies loved Emiliano.

Brando was bigger and tougher than the real Emiliano when Brando portrayed the rebel in *Viva Zapata*.[14] Emiliano was more suave and something of a country fop with his signature 55-gallon sombrero, handlebar moustache that almost took on a life of its own, and his cashmere gaucho trousers with silver buttons and bolero jackets of the *charro* horseman class of upper peasantry. Emiliano was perhaps an even better salesman than *Presidente* Fox would be later. Fox sold soft drinks and capitalism. Emiliano sold freedom—freedom to work the earth and inhabit the earth of the ancestors. True to his romantic ladies' man persona, Emiliano romanticized life just as well as death. Just as Hirohito would call on his followers to be willing to die for the Empire of the Rising Sun and go to heaven, Emiliano called on his original Zapatistas to be willing to die for the ancestral lands demarcated on Mexican maps as "Morelos."

Steinbeck, in preparation for penning the *Viva Zapata* screenplay, wrote that Emiliano "was a greater man than his people. He belongs to the whole world, and his symbol of piracy and violence, and of resistance against oppression, is a world symbol." There may be some truth to this seemingly racist remark, but Emiliano did little by himself, except ride into an obvious trap to meet his end at the bullet of an assassin. The working class people of Morelos and their exploitative

---

[14] John Steinbeck, *Zapata*. New York: Penguin, 1993, 15.

federal government ruling class enemies created Emiliano much more than he created them. The class struggle continues nearly a century after Emiliano's death and has even spread several thousand kilometers southeast from Morelos to Chiapas.

Emiliano's legacy is often remembered as *"Tierra y Libertad!"* which is a posthumous abbreviation of Emiliano's full rallying cry: *"Reforma, Libertad, Justicia y Ley!"* Reform, liberty, justice, and law all feature prominently in the 1911 Plan of Ayala, which schoolteacher Otilio Montaño Sánchez transcribed for the barely literate Zapata. Like unto the founding declaration of *Comandante* Ramona's *Ejercito Zapatista Liberacion Nacional (EZLN)*, the earlier Plan of Ayala (a) asserts a right to ancestral lands, (b) demands an end to the perpetration of violence on the people, (c) rejects the tyranny of corrupt federal government, and (d) denounces other former allies as having become traitors "for a fistful of coins." Unlike the later declarations of the *EZLN*, which reject Mexican federal government as an institution, The Plan of Ayala left the government structure largely intact but with key personnel changes. Unlike their former allies now turned traitors, Emiliano and the original Zapatistas did not seek coins—not even a mere fistful. The original Zapatistas and their chosen leader Emiliano sought land: land as nourishing mother; land as freedom; and land as justice.

The divide-and-conquer strategy of Porfirio Diaz in bribing other former Zapatista allies with a mere fistful of coins was neither new, nor is it forgotten. The current race-to-the bottom economic model of global capitalism allows money to flow freely across artificial political borders while creating physical fences, walls, and armed-force obstacles to the free flow of peoples. The leaders who, for their own fistful of coins, manage to sell out their constituents at the lowest price attract the free-flowing global capital investment to wage-enslave the population. The physical barriers to emigration become necessary, then, to keep the wage-slaves in the country where their leader and global capital can exploit them. The middle class, mostly in the United States and Europe, choose to hold on to their fistful of coins by largely ignoring the lower rungs of the socioeconomic ladder and, thus, participating in the worldwide Ponzi scheme as semi-preferred members.

The pure soul of humanity, however, is not full of coins; it is full of rebellion. The diminutive *Comandante* Ramona, well under five-feet, and the dandy Emiliano were full of rebellion. They were creations of their people and of all peoples. The soul wants, more than anything, to be free. As water flows always downward through the path of least resistance, the pure soul flows upward and outward through the path of greatest freedom. As other less soulful forces oppress humanity, the rebel soul of humanity rebels.

Although Mexico had declared independence from Spain in 1820, the 34-year presidency of Porfirio Diaz became ever more oppressive and ever more dominated by capitalists from the United States. The *hacendados* under Diaz came to usurp land and village throughout the country until ultimately dominating 81 percent in 1910. In the state of Oaxaca, home of Diaz and his predecessor, Benito Juarez, those living in the traditional communal society and remaining outside the hacienda system reduced to a pitiful 14.5 percent under Diaz.[15]

Nearly an octogenarian on September 15, 1910, Diaz orchestrated a centenary celebration of Mexico's struggle for independence from Spain on September 15, 1810. The public financed a nearly month-long patriotic siesta, and Diaz had invited dignitaries from across the globe to revel in Mexico City. Foreshadowing the Third Reich, Diaz arranged a pageant of 10,000 performers tracing the history of Mexico from the Aztecs all the way to Diaz. The guests enjoyed a ten-course meal and sixteen musical performances. The decadent festivities belied, however, the rampant poverty, unemployment, hunger, and poor public health of Mexico City, with its perennially flood-prone sewage system that was entirely inadequate for the nearly half-million inhabitants in 1910.

Few, if any, attending the party of the century in the *Distrito Federal* suspected any chance of revolution emerging from Zapata's neighboring state of Morelos, which was as thoroughly dominated by the hacienda system as any other state. Zapata's family had actually been *Porfiristas* in Morelos in the 1870s but had soured on the "supreme ruler" after Diaz ignored repeated complaints about the tyranny of the sugar kings of the haciendas and the related foreign investment and extraction.

Diaz had long successfully employed his *"pan o palo"* doctrine: "bread or the club," in which he beat or murdered any who stood in his way after he had unsuccessfully offered a bribe. His philosophy of bribery reduced to his favorite adage that the dog with a bone in his mouth neither steals nor bites.

---

[15] Adolfo Gilly, *The Mexican Revolution*. 2005, p. 40.

Diaz practiced his bone-in-mouth method on the press as well, with generous subsidies to publishers and editors friendly to Diaz. Conversely, journalists who criticized Diaz encounterd the club. Diaz also forced anti-sedition legislation through a toothless congress; pursuant to *ley mordaza* or the gagging law, police could summarily jail reporters and editors upon mere report from any citizen to the effect that the journalist-suspect "intended" unpatriotic expression. Worse still was the abolition of jury trial for any journalist so accused. Any federal magistrate, all of whom were appointed by Diaz, could rule on both fact and law in such cases, virtually assuring conviction of any dissident voices.

Zapata had earned a reputation as a first-rate horseman, if not bronco-buster, by 1910, also acquiring a battle-proven rifle from one uncle and a pair of coin-studded trousers from another. The latter gift was in tribute to *Los Plateados* or "Men of Silver" bandits who raided Morelos for decades on horseback. Zapata had long dreamt of overthrowing the *hacendados* and their patrons in the now festive *Distrito Federal*.

In the high Sonoran desert up north, Diaz had a formidable "Indian problem" with the ferocious Yaquis, part of whom made common cause with Francisco Madero in the November 1910 rebellion and part of whom remained enemies of all whites and *mestizos.* In addition, Diaz worried that Geronimo's excursions into Mexico may invite the United States so far south of the border as to entice the annexation of Sonora in order to quell the Apache "Indian problem" that was impeding western expansion of cattle ranches and white settlement in Arizona and New Mexico.

Shaman come Chief Geronimo hated Mexicans more than Americans due to the massacre of his wife and three children in 1850 at the hands of Mexican soldiers in Chiricahua. Geronimo and fellow Apache Chief Victorio continued to raid soldiers and civilians alike on both sides of the border for the majority of Diaz' tenure.

It was another semi-literate Mexican peasant, however, who would, perhaps, caused Diaz the most trouble of all. "Pancho" Villa was the illegitimate son of a sharecropper on the largest hacienda in the state of Durango. At the age of 16, Villa claimed to have shot *hacendado* Augustin Lopez Negrete for making advances at Villa's sister.[16] This, according to Villa, began his life of Robin Hood style social banditry; Villa soon learned the lessons of the wisdom of bribery in securing inordinately favorable treatment from magistrates who would preside over his indictments for cattle rustling. Diaz' henchman in the state, Luis Terrazas, was arguably more ruthless, greedy, and violent than Villa. Terrazas had earned a name for himself dispatching the Apaches when the vaunted United States Cavalry could not. He then went on, as governor, to appropriate estates of *hacendados* who had wound up on the wrong side of Napoloen's adventure, privatizing precious water resources in the high desert, taxing farms, fencing in previously free cattle range land, censoring the press, outlawing strikes, murdering dissidents, and selling off natural

---

[16] Frank McLynn, *Villa and Zapata: A History of the Mexican Revolution.* New York: Basic Books, 2000, 58.

resources to foreign capitalists. Life for the indigenous became increasingly more oppressive under Terrazas and Diaz. The era was ripe for a Mexican Robin Hood. Terrazas retired as governor of Chihuahua, though, in 1904 and passed the mantle to his even greedier and more ruthless son-in-law, Enrique Creel.

Villagers, especially those who did not speak Spanish, soon found their remaining lands expropriated by Creel, so these indigenous peoples became landless laborers at the mercy of a brutal, corrupt, and dictatorial governor who had gone as far as to abolish elections. The only consolation was that foreign investment had temporarily spurred the economy to the advantage of all, and there was ample employment for all who were willing and able to toil for the expropriating mine owners, ranchers, and farmers. By 1909, however, with Maderos mounting an electoral challenge to Diaz, the price of silver dropped on the world market, thus sending the state of Chihuhua into a depression with high unemployment; Creel exacerbated the situation by raising taxes on the lower class while leaving the *hacendados* and foreign investors virtually untaxed.

The macho and martial people of northern Mexico found in Villa an archetype of their culture. Villa was a skillful gunfighter and successful raider of haciendas, which were viewed by the villagers and peasants as stolen property. Villa, therefore, enjoyed a favorable popular reputation throughout his days of banditry. Once Madero had called for the November 1910 rebellion and Diaz had reacted unwisely both militarily and politically, northern Mexicans gravitated toward Villa, his charisma, his thorough knowledge of the mountains, his superior horsemanship, and his bravery in battle. Although originally subordinate to Orozco, Villa eventually rose to prominence by popular appeal. After early victories against federal troops and repeated successful raids against *hacendados*, Villa eventually gathered more and more disparate groups under one large tent of malcontents with various grudges and grievances against this or that authoritarian *Porfirista*. Rebels routinely freed prisoners from jail, destroyed tax records, and burned official land-grant archives. Any act of deconstructing the oppressive federal or state apparatus now claimed the protective mantle of the revolution.

All of this rebellion was much more than Madero had anticipated when he supplanted Monterrey General Bernardo Reyes to seek the presidency in 1910. Madero had become the electable alternative to continued dictatorship, though he had offered little or no solution to the problems of foreign debt, unemployment, dropping wages, and poor crop yields. Many previously separate factions had ultimately coalesced behind Madero with inherently competing demands of democratic reforms, higher standard of living for middle class bourgeoisies, union rights for workers, abolition of the hacienda system, and land reform. After languishing in prison while Diaz had himself re-elected, Madero fled to the United States and drew up his Plan of San Luis, which addressed only political reform in calling for a one-term presidency and land reform in a radical redistribution that would never fully come to fruition.

Returning to Mexico in February, Madero hoped to capitalize on the eventual May 1911 resignation of Diaz and self-exile in France. Days before leaving country, however, Diaz and Madero signed the Ciudad Juarez Accords, which ceded power to Francisco Leon de la Barra, then secretary of foreign affairs, who was to administer upcoming new elections. The rebels in the countryside were restless, though. Diaz and Madero had hoped to prevent further revolt by establishing a new government, but without the land reforms of the Plan of San Luis. The villagers throughout the country took matters into their own hands and reclaimed ancestral lands from the *hacendado* interlopers. Madero was as indecisive as he was impotent to prevent the revolution in the countryside that wrote a plan of its own while ignoring the Accords as if so much ink on paper.

Many of those villagers and peasants who had taken up arms on one side or other of the effort to oust Diaz did not lay down their arms after Diaz left the country. There was little work and almost no good work for most, and defending families and land, new or old, required a rifle—or so they believed at the time, much like unto many twenty-first century citizens of the United States. The revolt had been a long time coming, but came for many good reasons. The typical oppression and exploitation by an elite oligarchy of a largely disenfranchised working class and dispossessed farmers worsened almost yearly. Although the Spanish had invaded, conquered, and colonized Mexico, it was the native-born Diaz who pushed the *hacendado* system and its graft and corruption to an extreme. It is likely that rebellion was inevitable in at least Morelos and Chihuahua, even had the bourgeoisies of *Distrito Federal* not made common cause, but the convergence of disgruntled citizens and factions overwhelmed the federal and state governments for a decade of revolt.

Just as Diaz played his role in inciting rebellion, Villa and Zapata, too, played their roles. All three were native sons with mixed ancestry. All three were charismatic leaders, and all three were prone to violence. The people would likely have rebelled absent any one of these three, two of the three, or even all three; the circumstances may have been different, but the exploitation required by foreign capital investment would still have created untenable and inhuman conditions regardless of which particular man had been the nominal leader of this or that group.

True to the trichotomy of rebellion, a small group of oligarchs manipulated a system of government and economy that exploited the masses until resistance grew, eventually to a critical mass that ended, unfortunately, in violent civil war. The elite oligarchs employed the usual tactics of dividing to conquer, bribing and co-opting would-be opponents, and threats of violence as well as outright violence. In the end, the corruption built a house of cards that fell in on itself. The rebels hastened the disintegration of the government and eventually gained the support or tacit support of the masses, which created the opportunity for successful rebellion.

It is difficult to calculate the effect that the Mexican Revolution had on later life in Mexico, but the results spread deep and wide. The southern rebels of Morelos have yet to achieve their utopian Plan of Ayala land and self-governance reforms, but they never laid down their arms, even after the assassination of Zapata. It is not mere coincidence that the rebels further south in Chiapas in 1994 chose to name their

EZLN after the Morelos rebel leader. All Mexican presidents since the revolution have appropriately considered the peasants and Indians in their campaigns and initiatives. A century after the 1910 revolution, the Zapatistas in Chiapas openly maintain what they refer to as an autonomous zone of local governance. The class war rebellion, therefore, forever changed the social, political, and economic future of Mexico in ways that are obvious and real one-hundred-years later.

Too Corrupt Not to Fail

"We began planning the Revolutionary War in order to issue our own money again"

—Benjamin Franklin

Bank failures in the United States are nearly as old as the Constitution.

History of Major Bank Panics in United States	
Year	Cause
1819	First financial crisis in United States
1873	Depression in United States and Europe 101 failures
1907	Dow Jones Industrials fell over 50% 73 failures
1929-1934	Stock Market Collapse and Depression 806 failures
1989	S & L Crisis 534 failures—single year high
2008-2009	Recession 327 failures

Source: Federal Deposit Insurance Corporation

Before the Great Depression, there were bank panics in 1819, 1873, and 1907. Each led to widespread foreclosures, bankruptcies, and unemployment. So too, the recession of

2008 has brought bank panics, foreclosures, bankruptcies, and unemployment not known in generations. It is impossible to calculate how many banks would have failed in the 2008 to 2009 crisis had it not been for bailouts and Fed intervention beyond that.

Americans who do work in the twenty-first century, ironically, work longer hours than ever before and more than their counterparts in any country civilized enough to track hours worked. Wages, however, have remained stagnant, at best, but have not kept pace with inflation since the Volcker reign at the Federal Reserve Bank in the 1980s. The March 2011 Consumer Price Index rose published by the United States Bureau of Labor Statistics reported an increase of 2.7 percent over the preceding twelve months. Gasoline prices rose 14.7 percent in the preceding three months, and food 1.1 in the preceding month. The Bureau developed a new way of calculating inflation, though, in the post-Volcker era by offsetting higher costs of consumer items according to their improvement in technology so that the price of a more advanced car is adjusted to represent its added value over the less advanced car of the past. But, the family still pays a larger portion of annual income for the family car than decades ago, and simpler models are just not on the new car market. Moreover, wages during the recession of 2008, have remained flat and declined in some regions and occupations.

What is most emblematic of the undeclared Class War by the elite on the workers is the 62.5 percent increase in productivity from 1989 to 2010 in the United States with a mere 12 percent increase in hourly wages over the same period. The other 40.5 percent trickled up, quietly, to under-taxed corporate profits, which went partly to under-taxed dividends and un-taxable investments in foreign ventures such as wood harvesting in Brazil, consumer electronic factories in China, and customer service call centers in India. The same 40.5 percent could have been given to workers in wages, benefits, or vacation time; it could have been paid in higher corporate or capital gains taxes, or it could have been invested in the United States in new industry. It was a matter of political choice that it went, instead, to those who needed it least, and who have invested it, largely, in one bubble economy after another from Trump's casinos and country clubs, to the dot com bubble, to the housing bubble, and to the too-big-to-burst bubble of the derivative markets, which some estimate at $700 trillion in intentionally inscrutable financial instruments that have little or no intrinsic value whatever. Many derivatives are nothing more than bets, or worse, unsound debt fraudulenlty repackaged as sound assets.

During the 2012 presidential campaign, leading Republican candidate Mitt Romney enjoyed support from foreign and multinational banks, with whom he has dealt throughout his career, helping wealthy individuals move capital across borders to tax havens offshore. In an interesting contrast, candidate Ron Paul, who was a long shot once again, received much of his funding from active duty military. Among Romney's top donors were Credit Suisse, Wells Fargo, Barclays Bank of America, JP Morgan Chase and Company, and Citigroup. Like President Obama, Romney also received hundreds of thousands from executives at investment banking firm Goldman Sachs, who many blame for the derivatives and speculation that crashed the market and economy during the

Bush presidency. The 2016 Sanders campaign raised over $100 million from individual donors, contributing an average of $27 each.

Meanwhile, this derivatives market of wild speculation that some compare to casino gambling with an entire deck of wild-cards continues unabated and largely unregulated. Worse yet, is that many of these instruments are so complicated that the buyers of the "financially engineered" investments, as the bankers euphemize them, do not even understand what they are buying. While the deriviaties originally acted mostly as insurance against other, usually leveraged, investments, they have, over the years, mutated into more and more esoteric and obscure investments based on, or derived from, an underlying stock, bond, or other asset and often one other factor, such as weather, consumer price index, or unemployment rate. While there is some logic to hedging an investment in an insurance corporation against extreme weather patterns that may increase claims, the main concern with a derivative is that it is typically leveraged exponentially. This factor alone creates great uncertainty in the market with estimates of the entire derivatives market ranging from $600 trillion to over 1 quadrillion. These numbers are difficult to comprehend, but when compared to a federal budget of $700 billion, we see that that we are looking at a market with one thousand times that amount. JP Morgan Chase itself holds a portfolio of derivatives with a face value of over $79 trillion. Given an overall United States' economy of only $10 trillion and world economy of $65 trillion, a crashing derivatives market valued at over sixty times that would, obviously, wreak havoc all over the globe. Indeed, the notional value of the derivatives market is twenty-three-times world GDP, and ten times the value of every stock and bond on world markets.

Warren Buffet once referred to derivatives as "financial weapons of mass destruction." It is important to keep in mind that the derivative has little or no intrinsic value. It could not be cashed in for a hill of soybeans, factory machinery, or even the "good will" of an existing business name, such as Schwinn, which replaced the Pacific moniker of bicycles sold primarily at Target stores and manufactured entirely offshore. A derivative is nothing more than a lawful bet. Wall Street, however, focuses on commissions—the more it can sell and the higher the price, the higher the commission. The underlying value is irrelevant to agents, brokers, houses, and banks. Unfortunately, it is difficult to see an end in sight to derivatives, as they fill the portfolios of the ten top banks in the United States, and these same banks dominate 77 percent of all United States' banking assets. Both Republicans from John McCain and Sarah Palin to Barak Obama and most Democrats continue, unfortunately to cater to these powerful interests in the financial sector that has grown to over 20 percent of domestic GDP at the expense of a shrinking industrial base in the Unites States.

Perhaps more troubling is the intermingling and tangling of markets in the globalized economy wherein Bank of America usurped the FDIC and the Fed by investing in European derivative markets in London and Frankfurt—at the risk of the American taxpayer. Other "too big to fail" institutions are similarly situated. A 2012 *New York Times* article, "A Secretive Banking Elite Rules Trading in Derivatives" revealed that representatives from too-big JPMorgan Chase, Goldman Sachs,

Morgan Stanley, Bank of America and Citigroup met monthly in Midtown Manhattan to confer on how best to protect their derivative golden goose. While apologists for the financial industry claim that these acts are private and legal, it is important to remember that AIG and the insurance it provided to many of these instruments—instruments that brought AIG begging for a taxpayer bailout with little or no oversight, regulation, or benefit for the funders.

The corrupt and unpunished banks will bring increased volatility, much of it irrational, even amongst such vaunted concerns as the Dow Jones Industrial stocks that, inexplicably ranged from a 54 percent loss for Bank of America while American express gained over 14 percent in the same one-year period ending in mid-November 2011 during the previous edit of this book. This is not to mention the meteoric 21 percent rise for McDonald's and 24 percent rise for IBM, as listed below:

Dow Jones Industrial one-year change November 2010 to November 2011:

MMM 3M Company	-7.03%
AA Alcoa	-33.79%
AXP American Express	+14.63%
T AT&T	-0.99%
BAC Bank of America	-54.24%
BA Boeing	-0.48%
CAT Caterpillar	-2.22%
CVX Chevron	+14.05%
CSCO Cisco Systems	-8.26%
KO Coca-Cola Company	+2.13%
DD E I Du Pont	-5.01%
XOM Exxon Mobil	+6.54%

GE General Electric	-12.06%
HPQ Hewlett Packard	-37.02%
HD Home Depot	+6.08%
INTC Intel	+13.79%
IBM International Business Machines	+24.53%
JNJ Johnson & Johnson	+3.33%
JPM JPMorgan Chase	-22.77%
KFT Kraft Foods	+11.03%
MCD McDonalds	+21.03%
MRK Merck & Company	-3.75%
MSFT Microsoft	-5.55%
PFE Pfizer	+12.34%
PG Procter & Gamble	-1.73%
TRV Travelers Companies	+2.58%
UTX United Technologies Corporation	-1.77%
VZ Verizon Communications	+4.02%
WMT Wal-Mart Stores	+7.71%
DIS Walt Disney Company	-9.52%

Much of the rise and fall in these stock prices has little to do with the actual value of their company or market share in their industry or the future of the company or industry themselves, but rather results from speculation of future financial manipulation of the corporation by speculators and monetarists, who have dominated economies for centuries. The establishment of the Federal Reserve Bank in 1913 was a major monetarist accomplishment in privatization—indeed, privatizing the actual control of the nation's currency and monetary policy. Most recent attempts at privatizing this or that function of government are mild by comparison.

While Main Street remains awash in unemployed, underemployed, and uninsured, Wall Street has largely "recovered" from the great recession of 2008. Indeed, the Dow is healthy, and rising; profits of Fortune 500 companies are solid, and executive bonuses are back in the stratosphere. But what do the wizards of Wall Street and top corporate CEOs do for and with all that money? Why does the president of Home Depot earn 500 times that of a checker? What do hedge fund managers add to the economy? What do they make? What do they do?

They massage money.

In 2007, the financial sector accounted for nearly half of all corporate profits. The current preferred term on Wall Street for their machinations is "financial engineering," which suggests that something is being constructed. Of course the something recently constructed by these wizards was a house—of cards: a house of cards that collapsed on our housing market, bursting the bubble all over the country, and especially in the West. These financial "engineers" manage to extract hefty piles of cash from their construction "work," work that massages money to make more money, somehow magically, as if modern day alchemists spinning gold from hay.

Main Street knows more tragedy than magic with 15 million unemployed, approaching 50 million uninsured, and countless millions homeless or foreclosed upon by those too-big-to-fail banks of gilded Wall Street. Yet these money massagers are concerned, not about the unemployed, but about unemployment as lost marketing opportunities. We hear the laments on the evening news along with other concerning numbers, such as the burgeoning trade deficit, vulnerable government credit rating, the budget deficit, the national debt—about to hit the ceiling, and those entitlement programs. The entitlement programs such as Medicare and

Medicaid are particularly of concern because they are monies spent on social programs but also monies that are not available for engineering by Wall Street. The Social Security Fund is another concern, and all the more so after President Bush's failure to promote "personal accounts" that would do for America's pensions what insurance companies have done to health care, that is: create a corporate administration to charge management fees 20 percent higher than the current government administration costs. No doubt we will see the proposals again, once the Dow passes its 2008 heights; no doubt, too, we will hear the intellectually dishonest claims as to how inefficient and incompetent government is and how much better corporations could do at the same task. These calls for privatization and austerity have come not just from the Tea Party, but Democratic presidents as well.

Obama, veering right, but reportedly in the middle of the road, tries to appear less outrageous than Paul Ryan, but offers a budget only slightly less Malthusian in austerity-mania. The ultimate compromise between the president and the congress claimed $39 billion in discretionary cuts, which portend new, aggravated, and prolonged misery for seniors, poor, and students.

The world astounded at the failure of the Joint Select Committee on Deficit Reduction, affectionately known as "The Super Committee," and there is much talk of "job creation," "fiscal responsibility," and "balance."

But one thing is assured: the class war continues and is likely to worsen in 2016.

Nobel laureate Paul Krugman and other leading economists continue to urge that we loosen Wall Street's grip on Washington and state capitols, re-instate Glass-Steagall and similar banking regulation, including banning derivatives as well as the now entirely legal insider trading of United States senators and representatives. The banking and finance industry—especially the "too big to fail" houses, do not have America's interests in mind when they gamble on risky investments, knowing that they can go to the congress they have bought and paid for to insist on favorable legislation to save them from their own misdeeds. This must stop. In the meantime, Former Housing and Urban Development economist Catherine Austin Fitts wisely recommends that we hold our savings in local, community institutions that will invest our money in local projects instead of gambling our money in the derivatives market.

Nguyễn and the Patriots

Hồ Chí Minh repeatedly petitioned President Truman for support.

Truman, as had President Wilson, ignored Hồ Chí Minh, but that was when Hồ went by the name his father donned him at age ten: "Nguyễn the Accomplished," which Hồ later changed to "Nguyễn the Patriot," and, ultimately, Hồ Chí Minh. After these two presidential rebuffs, Hồ, ironically, quoted earlier United States Presidents on September 2, 1946 when he delivered the Vietnamese Declaration of Independence, which began:

> 'All men are created equal. They are endowed by their Creator with certain inalienable rights, among these are life, liberty, and the pursuit of happiness.' This immortal statement was made in the Declaration of Independence of the United States of America m 1776. In a broader sense, this means: All the peoples on the earth are equal from birth, all the peoples have a right to live, to be happy and free.

Several years later, President Eisenhower quietly estimated that Hồ would have won by 80% had the pan-Vietnam election not been pre-empted by the French and U.S. governments. Hồ, while often denigrated as a charlatan, opportunist, or political chameleon, managed to out-imagine and out-philosophize his detractors and opponents in a manner rivaled only by Fidel Castro. Hồ convincingly melded French Revolution ideals with raw Marxism and Confucian ethics with seamless felicity and aplomb in his own brand of class war.[17] In perhaps the

---

[17] William Duiker, *Ho Chi Minh: A Life*. New York: Hyperion, 2000, 564.

greatest testament to his cause as opposed to his personality, the people of Vietnam fought on well after Hồ's death in 1969, ultimately repeling the invading United States military, reunifying their country, and instituting their own brand of communism that continues to evolve today.

On behalf of the Group of Vietnamese Patriots, Hồ published the following demands to the Paris Peace Conference through the socialist newspaper *L'Humanite* on June 18, 1919:

> General amnesty for all native political prisoners;
>
> Reform of Indochinese just by granting the natives the same judicial guarantees as were enjoyed by Europeans:
>
> Freedom of press and opinion;
>
> Freedom of association;
>
> Freedom of emigration and foreign travel;
>
> Freedom of instruction and the creation in all provinces of technical and professional schools for indigenous people;
>
> Replacement of rule by decree with rule of law;
>
> Election of a permanent Vietnamese delegation to the French Parliament, to keep it informed of the wishes of the people.

Although his principles and logic were undeniable, Hồ's timing and sense of what was possible left much to be desired. After a protracted war on French soil that had filled the cemeteries and drained the treasury, the colonies in Algeria, Cambodia, and Vietnam were viewed by the French as resources to exploit rather than peoples to respect, much less liberate.[18]

The French, of course, did not liberate Indochina. In 1946, amidst threats of escalation of tensions between the Vietnamese and the French occupiers, Hồ warned *New York Times* correspondent David Schoenbrun that the Vietminh would crouch in the jungle like tigers waiting for nightfall to attack the French elephant and tear it to pieces. Hồ's was an apt simile for the jungle warfare the Vietnamese so successfully employed against both the French and the Americans for nearly three decades.

The tigers were no more effective than they were during the *Tết* Offensive of 1968. The military campaign intended to end the war in Vietnam by launching a series of battles beginning on January 31 against the United States armed forces and their Republic of Vietnam allies. The People's Army of Vietnam, from the north, and the National Liberation Front (NLF) for South Vietnam, or Viet Cong, hoped to spark a general uprising among the population, thereby toppling the U.S. puppet regime in Saigon.

Tết Nguyên Đánthe is the traditional first day of the lunar, and the most important holiday in Vietnamese culture and history. Both North and South Vietnam had announced that there would be a general cease-fire in observance of the national holiday. The *Tết Mậu Thân* (Tet, year of the monkey), however, was anything but peaceful. The NLF launched a wave of morning attacks that they redoubled the next morning with more than 80,000 communist troops striking hundreds of villages and towns, including 36 provincial capitals, as well as

---

[18] Sophie Quinn-Judge, *Ho Chi Minh: The Missing Years*. Berkeley: University of California Press, 2002, 12.

Saigon itself in a stunning display of resolve that caught the United States forces by surprise due to both the scope and boldness of the campaign. The Battle of Huế lasted over a month and claimed the lives of thousands of residents executed as traitors by the NLF. The NLF attack on the strategic United States combat base at Khe Sanh lasted over two months before the NLF exacted hundreds of American casualties, who gained nothing from the battle, much to the great dismay of the military commanders and civilian leadership in Washington D.C.

The effect on morale stateside was devastating. Walter Cronkite, the most trusted name in broadcast news, announced that the war in Vietnam had become "unwinnable." President Johnson is reported to have lamented in response, "If I've lost Cronkite, I've lost Middle America." LBJ had also lost any chance at re-election. The Democratic National Convention that year, even without LBJ running for re-election, was the site of the most debilitating civil unrest in the United States since the Civil War or Revolution.

The communist leadership in Hanoi, consistent with the trichotomy of rebellion, had persuaded enough countrymen to support the General Offensive and General Uprising to "Crack the Sky, Shake the Earth,"[19] and expel the invading Americans. The decision to launch the bold offensive followed years of fierce debate among party leaders. One faction opposed the plan as it threatened the economy of North Vietnam; another faction preferred reunification through political means; the

---

[19]Clark Dougan, et al., *Nineteen Sixty-Eight.* Boston: Boston Publishing Company, 1983, 10.

third, hard-liner faction urged decisive military action against an enemy that was losing support at home and was alienating the "hearts and minds" of village after village in South Vietnam.

The aerial bombing of North Vietnam was destroying infrastructure, inflicting massive casualties, and depleting Hanoi's resources. Hồ and the "centrist" communists proposed the "fighting while talking" plan as a compromise. Imitating their opponents, the militant faction arrested hundreds of political adversaries in 1967 so as to solidify their position, initiate their strategy, and put an end to "dovish calls for talks, criticism of military strategy, Chinese diatribes of Soviet perfidy, and Soviet pressure to negotiate—all of which needed to be silenced."[20] Hồ, despite losing the debate, remained in a position of leadership in Hanoi.

The price the communists paid for the operation was bloody and sobering. The North suffered nearly a 50% casualty rate of the 90,000 total troops deployed. United States General Wheeler, though, admitted that to for all intents and purposes, the V.C. now controlled the countryside, and the State Department determined that U.S. loss of control had "made pacification virtually inoperative. In the Mekong Delta the Vietcong was stronger now than ever and in other regions the countryside belongs to the VC."[21]

---

[20] Nguyen, Lien-Hang Nguyen, "The War Politburo: North Vietnam's Diplomatic and Political Road to the Tet Offensive." (*Journal of Vietnamese Studies*1, 2006), 1-2.

[21] David Schmitz, *The Tet Offensive: Politics, War, and Public Opinion.* Westport CT: Praeger, 2004, 109.

The villages were old battle fronts for the communists. Shortly after the Geneva conference of 1954 and the unsuccessful attempts to hold national elections or peacefully reunify the country, Hanoi embarked on a new land reform program consistent with its slogan to "build the North, look to the South." Hồ had earlier proposed radical land reform during the war with the French but had tempered it some after consultations with Beijing. The plan was to convert all cultivable land to the collective system after the Chinese model. Hanoi promised to convert the "land to the tiller" in the northern provinces. The promise pursued both economic and political goals. The economic goal was to increase productivity by transferring "excess" land from wealthy villagers to the landless peasants. The theory was that the new land owners would work harder than the formers owners, thus increasing production. The pursuit of this economic goal would, as a matter of course, further a political goal of dismantling the feudal village landlord system. Rural leadership councils comprised of the new peasant land owners would replace the landlords and, presumably, naturally carry out Communist Party policies out of both self-interest and gratitude.

Hồ bluntly referred to the land reform as "class struggle" at a cadre conference in 1954, advising that "In the village, the most important task is to remake rural organizations: the administrative committee, the guerilla militia, the associations for peasants, youth, and women." He further admonished that Party members should apply the appropriate sanction to opposition, denouncing torture as a "savage method used by imperialists, capitalists, and feudal elements to master the masses and the revolution."[22]

Savagery, unfortunately, ensued and continued throughout the next two decades. True to Mao's dictum that "revolution is not a dinner party," the battle for land reform was long and brutal, not fully attempted until after the last Americans evacuated Saigon in 1975. Local councils executed thousands of landlords during the reforms, some unfairly, given their generally good conduct before and during the "class struggle." Other villagers who attempted to defend their former landlords, often for just cause, met a similar savage fate of torture and or execution.

Torture and execution were also widely committed by the United States forces and their ARVN allies in the south. The Phoenix Project was the formalization of a *"contre coup"* philosophy of the CIA that the war was more a political than military struggle with 5 per-cent of the population promoting communism, another 5 per-cent promoting American-style capitalism, and the 90 per-cent majority wanting peace and prosperity. True to the trichotomy of rebellion, the communist faction had begun to win the "hearts and minds" of the majority and, thus, win the war. Eventually, the hearts and minds were enough, and Vietnam became re-unified, communist (after a fashion), and independent. In early response to the successes of the communists, CIA Saigon Station Chief, Peer DeSilva, created a small cadre of "counter-terror teams," tasked to "bring danger and death to the

---

[22]Hồ Chí Minh, "Speech at the Recapitulative Meeting of the Second Phase of Land Reform, Thai Nguyen" (1954).

Vietcong functionaries themselves, especially in areas where they felt secure." His rationale was that "The Vietcong were monstrous in the application of torture and murder to achieve the political and psychological impact they wanted." America, then, would match or outmatch the savagery of the communists.

Hồ estimated that with two Vietcong cadre in each hamlet, the communists could win the war, no matter how many soldiers the Americans brought. The object of *Contre Coup*, and later the Phoenix Project, was to identify and terrorize each and every Vietcong cadre, their families, and any sympathizers. The operation began in 1964 in what the CIA called "Provincial Interrogation Centers." Pacific Architects and Engineers, an American contractor, built a total of 44 interrogation centers—one in each province in South Vietnam. Special police forces used abuse, coercion, and torture to identify Vietcong at every level, region, city, village, and hamlet. In some cases entire families became assassination targets. Province Interrogation Center Program Chief Robert Slater explained that, "the District Party Secretary usually does not sleep in the same house or even hamlet where his family lived, to preclude any injury to his family during assassination attempts."[23] The CIA had identified the District Party Secretary as key targets of the *Contre Coup* and Phoenix Project campaigns when it officially launched its Phoenix Program in the summer of 1967—seven months before the Têto ffensive. The plan seemed more reasonable than the previous tactics; the new tactics were to

[23] Robert Slater "The History, Organization and Modus Operandi of the Viet Cong Infrastructure." Defense Intelligence School, 1970.

replace indiscriminate bombings, free-fire zones, and random search and destroy missions with specifically targeted assassinations. But as Navy SEAL Lieutenant Wilbur realized in the field, "we never really knew who the VC district chief was... you may have to isolate an agent out there and set in motion an operation that may not culminate for six months. It was much easier to go out and shoot people."[24] This new tactic was part of larger "winning the hearts and minds" initiative that had been a miserable failure up to this point. How selective, or not-so-selective, according to Lieutenant Wilbur, assassinations were going to win any heart or mind was never explained, if ever even considered. This approach would be analogous to Chinese occupying forces shooting state governors and their families in order to persuade mainstream Americans to welcome Beijing-style communism in the United States. During congressional hearings in 1970, the veteran Representative from New York, Ogden Reid, noted that "if the Union had had a Phoenix program during the Civil War, its targets would have been civilians like Jefferson Davis or the mayor of Macon, Georgia."

The mechanics of a Phoenix operation were as simple as they were brutal. South Vietnamese secret police and military officers would torture a suspected Vietcong sympathizer for days, weeks, or months until the victim, correctly or incorrectly, named all fellow travelers and provided their whereabouts. The CIA would then dispatch an assassination team, sometimes Navy SEALS, sometimes Marine Reconnaissance teams, sometimes Army Special Forces.

[24]Douglas Valentine, *The Phoenix Program*. William Morrow and Company 1990, 171.

Former Governor of Nebraska, Bob Kerrey, lead one such team in Thanh Phong.

Kerrey's team accepted and completed their mission in February 1969—one year after the Tết offensive. Kerrey's mission, killing approximately 20 civilians, amounted to only a small fraction of the carnage, though. In the year of 1969 alone, the Phoenix Program claimed the lives of over 20,000 South Vietnamese, with over 100,000 tortured in the interrogation centers to achieve that end. Hallowed and decorated Vietnam veteran Colonel David Hackworth acknowledged that "there were thousands of such atrocities," going on to confess that his own unit had perpetrated "at least a dozen such horrors."

The most infamous Phoenix operation came to me known as the My Lai Massacre, in which United States Army Lieutenant Calley ordered the slaughter of 504 women and children. The total would have been higher, and the incident likely would never have come to light had not been for the intervention of helicopter pilot Warrant Officer One Hugh Thompson, who landed his craft between the soldiers and the remaining would-be victims. Perhaps the most outrageous charge brought against Calley in his Courts Martial was Specification 4:

> In that First Lieutenant William L. Calley, Jr. did, at My Lai 4, QuangNgai Province, Republic of South Viet-Nam, on or about 16 March 1968, with premeditation, murder one Oriental human being, an occupant of the village of My Lai 4, approximately two years old, by shooting him with a rifle.

Although Hugh Thompson did not testify at the trial, the testimony of United States Army photographer Sergeant Ronald Haeberle was as chilling as his widely distributed photographs:

> They were sitting in their kind of squat. First there were five soldiers standing in front of the group. The people were all sitting there facing north. Then three of the GI's walked off into the distance. Then I heard automatic fire. I looked back. The automatic fire was coming from one of the two soldiers. He was firing toward the people. Some of the people were trying to get up and run. They couldn't and fell down. This one woman, I remember, she stood up and tried to make it–tried to run–with a small child in her arms. But she didn't make it.

In his defense, Calley's attorney asked:

> Did you form any impression as to whether or not there were children, women, or men, or what did you see in front of you as you were going on?

The Lieutenant replied:

> I never sat down to analyze it, men, women, and children. They were enemy and just people.

In an earlier exchange, Calley explained:

> If I had -- questioned an order, I was supposed to carry the order out and then come back and make my complaint later.

The first to investigate the war crime was then 31-year-old Army Major Colin Powell, later to rise to Chairman of the Joint Chiefs of Staff and Secretary of State. In his report, Powell wrote the incredulous apology that, "In direct refutation of this portrayal is the fact that relations between American soldiers and the Vietnamese people are excellent."[25] A subsequent investigation by General Peers found that of the estimated 200 Vietnamese men, women, and children killed, only three or four were confirmed Vietcong. Calley himself never made any complaint about his Phoenix operation orders, and although he was potentially facing hundreds of years in jail, or capital punishment, for "following orders," the judge sentenced Calley to 20 years of hard labor after his military jury convicted him of the premeditated murder of 22 infants, children, women, and old men, and of assault with intent to murder a child of 2 years of age. Calley ultimately served less than five months due to intervention by President Nixon. The story of the My Lai Massacre shocked America and earned Seymour Hersh a Pulitzer Prize, but to the Vietnamese, it was an all too familiar occurrence—albeit an atrocious one.

The Vietnamese learned from several invasions by the Chinese, and over a century of French colonialism that revolution was, indeed, no dinner party. The people of Vietnam had developed their own brand of rebellion with political, guerilla, and terror tactics, some as brutal as their invaders. As early as 1845, Vietnamese rebels retaliated for the French Navy shelling Da Nang City by confiscating the property of the French Catholic Church, drowning several Jesuit priests, and cutting in half, lengthwise, Vietnamese Catholic converts.

Rebellion became a part of the Vietnamese culture through generations of history. As is typical with warfare and

---

[25] Robert Parry and Norman Solomon, "Behind Colin Powell's Legend," *The Consortium for Independent Journalism*, July 22, 1996.

revolution, the civilians, especially the lower class, suffered most. True to the trichotomy of rebellion, though, the Vietnamese masses found themselves in the middle of a struggle between an exploitative elite and a charismatic, if not ruthless, rebel class. In Vietnam, the hearts and minds went to the latter, eventually with success, much as we see in 2016 with the resurgence of the Taliban and the rise of ISIL.

Corporate Slavery

"These men have the most terrible, the most imperious of masters, that is, need. They must therefore find someone to hire them, or die of hunger. Is that to be free?"

—Simon Linguet, 1763

Corporations Paying No Federal Income Taxes

2005 tax year			
	Number	Percent	Average Receipts in millions
Foreign Controlled	38,483	65.2	$11.30
U.S. Controlled	1,263,726	66.7	$1.65

Source: United States Government Accountability Office

The corporation is now more a person than ever, according to our Supreme Court in *Citizen's United*,[26] which also further established the notion that money is speech. Given the context of the average $5 million senate campaign, the concept that money is speech is a dangerous affront to the principle of one

[26] See www.ClassWar2012.com for a complete copy of the actual decision.

person one vote. *Citizen's United* perverts the electoral process into a one dollar per vote. Those with the most money, therefore, own the government, by purchasing it. Since corporations, now considered persons, comprise the most wealth and spend the most money on campaign contributions, corporations have engineered a new form of slavery.

In the Americas, it began with Columbus, if not before him. Franciscan brother and fellow traveler Las Casas protested the exploitation by Columbus of the new colonies with its genocide and slavery that came with the imperialism of conquest by violence that is as much a hallmark of Western Civilization as science or reason.

Columbus' expedition was a charter from the crown of Spain. This charter system established the slave trade in the Americas that constituted perhaps the most brutal form of class war other than genocide: slavery. It was not successfully challenged for over a century, until the rebellions in the Caribbean.

Tacky had been a Coromantee chief before abducted into slavery. Until the Haitian Revolution of 1790, the revolt known as Tacky's War was the most significant slave rebellion in the Caribbean. Tacky and his Coromantee marched inland from St. Mary to invade the plantations and slaughter the white slave owners; Tacky's ultimate goal was to establish an African kingdom on Jamaica. As often befalls rebel leaders, Tacky died at the hands of vengeful authorities who made an example of him by displaying his severed head prominently atop a tall pole in Spanish Town. As a martyr, however, Tacky lived on to inspire later rebels who, eventually, overthrew slavery and colonial rule.

Tacky and the Coromantee were from Guinea in West Africa, which was the center of the eighteenth-century slave trade. Upon arrival in Jamaica, Tacky rose to a position of authority as an overseer. The Easter 1760 rebellion was a planned and timed event, with chosen targets and preliminary objectives of commandeering gun powder, shot, and firearms from Fort Haldane, where a single keeper guarded the British armory. The British had recently captured nearly every Caribbean island in the midst of the Seven Years' War with the Spanish and French. Despite a combined enemy, the British Navy prevailed with its superior ships, tactics, and forces. The British sought the rich natural resources of the Caribbean islands and their potential for cash crop agriculture such as sugar and coffee. Most consumers in Europe and America either supported, tolerated, or naïvely ignored the slave labor exploited to produce, process, and transport the goods.

Tacky's rebel party had grown to several hundred slaves by dawn. After early successes attacking white settlers still sleeping, the rebels paused to celebrate at Ballard's Valley. A slave from one of the overrun plantations turned against his people and sounded the alarm to summon a militia of eighty horsemen. Once word arrived to the Governor, he dispatched two companies of Scott's Hall Maroons who had joined forces with the British colonists as a condition of a peace treaty.

Shaman-like Obeahmen led the rebels on to battle, claiming that their powers would not allow them die. The British learned of this superstition and publicly hanged several captured Obeahmen to dishearten the rebels by destroying the mythology. This effort succeeded in discouraging many slaves, who returned to their former plantations. Tacky and the remaining two dozen or so hardliners retreated to the mountains, where the Maroons tracked them, assassinated Tacky, and chased his followers into a cave where they committed suicide to avoid capture and the certain punishment to follow.

Tacky and his rebels inspired later slave revolts throughout Jamaica. In the months that followed, as many as 400 slaves and 70 whites died in the unrest. In an attempt to terrorize the slaves back into submission, the British burned two slave ringleaders alive and locked two others in iron cages to publicly starve them to death. The brutality, however, only postponed the inevitable.

In 1765, Coromontee slaves rose again in St. Mary from a secret society that sealed their allegiance by drinking a mixture of rum, grave dirt, blood, and gunpowder. A zealous convert named Blackwell set a sugar mill ablaze at the Whitehall Estate, killed a white man and chased other whites to Ballard's Valley, where one white shot a rebel slave attempting to set fire to another plantation house. The remaining rebels retreated and were mostly captured and killed.

In 1766, still more Coromantee slaves staged yet another rebellion at Westmoreland Estate. The exact results of this insurgency is unclear, but another Coromantee soon after in Kingston was stopped before the slave girl intellectual-author could bring to fruition her plans to bomb a prominent public building in order to initiate a rebellion.

By 1804, while the new United States recently condoned slavery in its 1787 constitution, a former slave, Jean-Jacques Dessalines, who had led the successful revolts beginning in

1791, declared Haiti a free and independent country. This was the first former slave island to free itself from colonial rule. Others would follow, even the United States would only maintain slavery for 61 more years.

Socialists, however, saw a close relationship between what they referred to as chattel slavery, in which a person is bought and sold as an animal or piece of property, and wage slavery, in which workers rented themselves to capitalists. The concept of wage slavery goes back to biblical times, with such philosophers as Cicero arguing against the inherent problems with it.

Given that most Americans currently work for small and large corporations and almost all politicians are beholden to corporations, slavery has evolved into a new form: corporate slavery. With such bizarre Supreme Court decisions as *Citizens United*, in which corporate personhood was taken to frightening new heights, and *Diamond v. Chakrabarty*, in which the Supreme Court first established a corporation's right to hold a patent to a life form, corporations methodically paved the way for patenting of human life.

A genetic-science corporation and the University of Utah Foundation have recently patented two genes that relate to breast cancer and ovarian cancer. The American Civil Liberties Union and the Public Patent Foundation challenged the patent, and the case came before the Federal Circuit Court in April of 2011. The corporation's website describes the business as being "Founded in May 1991, Myriad Genetics' strategy is to understand the role of genes in human disease and then use that information to develop and commercialize products that assess a person's risk of developing disease...."

Myriad and the University of Utah Foundation argue that their patents encourage and reward biomedical research by attracting private investment. The American Civil Liberties Union and the Public Patent Foundation counter that allowing such patents restrict science and impair access to medical care.

The CEO of Myriad earned a B.A. and M.B.A. from the University of Utah and received honorary doctorates in engineering and science. The Board boasted one Nobel laureate and former Harvard professor, Walter Gilbert, but the remainder were primarily big pharma corporate insiders and heavyweights.

The important issue, though, is not one of science or business, but morality. Who are these people to patent the essence of nature? How can they stake claim to royalties on the basic building blocks to life just because they were first to isolate and name them? Should Polynesian sailors have held patent to the Pacific Ocean since they were the first to navigate it? Should Ptolemy have held patent to China, since he was the first Westerner to map it? Should James Brown hold patent to funk?

Moreover, what is the limit to this? Will Genentech charge a royalty for everyone who enjoys genetic immunity to AIDS should Genentech be the first to discover, name, and patent such a gene? Could some other global genetic conglomerate charge royalties from anyone with black hair, green eyes, above-average height, or a dulcet voice timbre? How far will the ruling class or ownership class go to exploit their technological pound-of-flesh taking? Will the privatization of education lead to corporate schools eventually patenting all knowledge they impart on their students later to charge royalties each time their alumni put the knowledge to use for profit? Will the Vatican corporatize and modernize its selling-of-indulgences-for-sins model to instead charge parishioners for answered prayers?

One day, a global conglomerate may gain control of the majority of the staple crops in the world food market. Or has this already happened? Monsanto has laid claim to a large portion of the more common agricultural seed stock, thus granting them royalties on much of the food that is grown around the world. It is troublesome to consider the powers of a corporation that controls the majority of human sustenance.

Slavery and serfdom were both commonplace during the first Dark Ages. Many in the slow food movement are beginning to demand an end to this corporate lust for power before corporations relegate humans to serfdom, if not outright chattel slavery. The first Renaissance, eventually, ended both affronts to humanity.

In order to bring on a second renaissance, Occupy and other protests are challenging police-state tactics and practices. The practice of video recording police misconduct is beginning to make the code of silence obsolete, and the ACLU Mobile Justice app for cell phones has made it easier than ever to record share, and post the state-sanctioned violence it with the media, and federal authorities, including the FBI, much to the chagrin of the corporatists, who want control of, not freedom for the people.

Children of the Casbah

Saâdi Yacef was an illiterate baker before the battle of Algiers.

Later in life, Yacef attained the office of Senator in Algeria's Council of the Nation, where he served for decades. During the Algerian war for independence from colonial invader France, Yacef was a key leader of Algeria's National Liberation Front (FLN). Before the war, Yacef had trained as an apprentice baker, to which working class vocation he returned upon repatriating to Algiers from France in 1952. In 1954, Yacef joined the FLN and rose to the position of military chief of the *Zone Autonome d'Alger*, or Autonomous Zone of Algiers. On September 24, 1957, French paratroopers captured Yacef, tortured him, and claimed to have turned him against Ali Ammar, a.k.a., Ali la Pointe, by revealing the whereabouts of this other FLN commander. Yacef denied the accusation, but somehow escaped a death sentence imposed while in custody. French paratroopers searched the Casbah district of Algiers for Ammar until they ultimately bombed him out of his hideout in a Casbah home of FLN sympathizers.[27] Amar, or Ali la Pointe as he was known by other children of Casbah, was no baker. Ammar was a pimp.

Ammar broke out of the infamous Barberousse prison in 1954 after the FLN recruited him to serve as a field commander. Ammar's most notorious act as commander was his 1956 assassination of the Mayor of Algiers, Amedee Froger. In retaliation, French paratroopers under the leadership of Colonel Yves Godard hunted Ammar down into a house in the Casbah where they offered Ammar the option to surrender;

---

[27]Ted Morgan, *My Battle of Algiers*. (2005), p.234

when he refused, the paratroopers bombed the "safe" house, killing Ammar and two dozen other children of the Casbah, presumably FLN sympathizers.

The FLN formed as a network of several paramilitary networks under the aegis of the Revolutionary Committee of Unity and Action, which followed the tradition of the Algerian People's Party. Two years into the War for Independence nearly all Algerian nationalist groups made common cause with the FLN. By 1956 the only important nationalist organization remaining outside the FLN was the *Mouvement National Algérien* (MNA) under Messali Hadj, who had resisted out of spite. Hadj had expected a more prominent role than offered and the FLN initially ignored him, much to their later dismay in the Café Wars for the loyalty of expatriates in France. Hadj boasted impressive nationalist credentials, having been elected the leader of the Algerian Workers Association in 1927. The FLN, however, readily subdued the MNA in Algeria and much less so in France. The FLN organized itself as a provisional government with a five-man combined executive and legislative body divided in six *wilayas*on, the territorial boundaries established during Ottoman rule.[28] The FLN named their military wing the *Armée de Libération Nationale* (ALN), which divided into small guerilla units fighting in the countryside as well as the city. Early efforts included two enemies: fellow nationalists of the MNA under Hadj, and the more formidable French colonizers.

---

[28]S. N. Millar, "Arab Victory: Lessons from the Algerian War (1954-62)," (*British Army Review Number 145,* Autumn 2008), 49.

Colonialism was well known in Algeria, even in antiquity when the area went by the name of "Numidia," founded by inhabitants who became known as the "Berbers."[29] The Berbers were accomplished cavalrymen and eventually cast off the Carthaginians during the Punic Wars of second and third centuries B.C., but only to fall under the yoke of the Roman Empire until its collapse in the fifth century A.D., which brought Byzantine colonialism until the Arabs invaded during the eighth century A.D. The Berbers, however, maintained their strength and some autonomy during the Middle Ages in Maghreb, Sudan, Andalusia, Mali, and Egypt.

The Spanish came in 1510 to replace Islam with Catholicism, but the Ottoman Empire began expanding into Algeria in 1517, ultimately displacing the Spaniards in 1529 until their return in 1732 with the armada of the Duke of Montemar. During Ottoman rule, corsairs pirated American and other ships sailing the Mediterranean, which led to the first and second Barbary Wars from 1801 to 1815 and a mention in the United States Marines Hymn celebrating victory on "the shores of Tripoli." The Ottoman corsairs preyed upon non-Muslim ships and often forced captives into slavery. Some corsair *jihads* even ventured ashore to Western European ports of call in pursuit of booty.[30] The raids nearly emptied the southern coasts of France, Italy, and Spain and claimed over one million casualties and victims of slavery.

---

[29] Michael Brett & Elizabeth Fentress, *The Berbers*. Oxford: Wiley-Blackwell, 1997, 29.

[30] A. B. C. Whipple, *To the Shores of Tripoli: The Birth of the U.S. Navy and Marines*, (Washington D.C.: Naval Institute Press, 2001).

The French eventually responded, on the pretext of a minor diplomatic impropriety rather than the piracy and slavery, by invading Algiers in 1830. For the next four decades, the French invaders with their violence and spread of disease decimated the native population by over thirty percent. The conquest ended with the defeat of the nomadic Tuareg peoples, after whom Volkswagen has named, with creative spelling, its 450-horsepower sport utility vehicle with Porsche engine.

Settlers in the new colony took full advantage of the confiscated communal land commandeered by the French government. The Tunisian plains are well-suited to modern agricultural practices with their temperate climate, abundant water sources, and relatively flat topography. The re-distribution of land to outsiders devastated many Algerian communities to the extent that the national literacy rate dropped measurably during this epoch due to the closure of Algerian schools. The current literacy rate (defined as adults who can read and write) in Algeria is 75%, equivalent to many poor rural areas and many inner cities of the United States.[31]

The Casbah is a city on a hill within the city of Algiers founded on the ruins of the trading post known in the Phoenecian and Carthagenian periods as Icosium. Greek legend held that twenty companions of Hercules founded the site, thus they named it after the ancient Greek word *Ικοσιον*, which derives from *εικοσι*, ancient Greek for "twenty." The original Punic settlers as early as the third century B.C. called it Al Jaza'ir, الجزائر, Arabic for "the islands." The Casbah of today includes masonries and mosques from the seventeenth century

---

[31] United Nations Development Program (http://www.undp.org)

in an extremely high density population district of labyrinthine alleys and lanes flanked by two and three story dwellings. The FLN from 1954 to 1962 chose the Casbah as their headquarters, safe haven, and breeding ground during the Algerian War for Independence.

The French responded to the FLN in the Casbah with brutal measures. Brigadier General Paul Aussaresses, veteran of World War II and the First Indochina War, admitted in a 2001 memoir that Paris ordered him to torture, execute, and violently break strikes in Algiers. Aussaresses insisted that then Minister of Justice and later 21st President of the Republic of France, François Mitterrand, knew full well the nature and extent of the campaign as well as its methods. Aussaresses first asserted his allegations in *Le Monde* in 2000, later on CBS *60 Minutes,* and more fully in his 2001, The Battle of the Casbah, in which he wrote that his orders were to"liquidate the FLN as quickly as possible."[32]

Aussaresses steadfastly justified his use of torture as a necessary evil in defeating terrorism by extracting intelligence quickly. The General also described his extensive use of *"escadrons de la mort,"* or death squads in Algiers. These confessions landed Aussarres on the docket in 2003 on trial for war crimes. The tribunal ultimately fined Aussaresses 7,500 Euros, and the Ministry of Defense stripped him of his rank, his *Légion d'honneur*, and forbade him to wear his uniform. Aussares denounced the punishments as hypocritical and

---

[32]Aussaresses, General Paul. *The Battle of the Casbah: Terrorism and Counter-Terrorism in Algeria, 1955-1957.* New York, Enigma Books, 2010.

asserted that torture should be employed in the War on Terror against Al Qaeda, as Cheney and Neocons agreed.

The trouble began in March of 1955 with the arrest of FLN leader Rabah Bitat. The recently released Abane Ramdane left prison with a mandate to revive the FLN after the loss of Bitat, which mandate Ramdane executed by violent uprising in Philippeville on August 20 of that same year. The next year the United Nations Security Council took up the "Algerian question." Ramdane and compatriot Larbi Ben M'Hidi called a Congress of Summam (*Congrès de La Soummam*), at which they decided to escalate the conflict by taking the fight to the capital. Meanwhile, the disloyal opposition of Algerian separatists calling themselves the "*Union françaisenord-africaine*" took over 70 lives by bomb on the road to Thèbes road in the Casbah while emissaries met secretly in Rome and Belgrade with French representatives of the Guy Mollet government to negotiate "peace."

As talks degenerated, Mollet withdrew from negotiations and M'Hidi advanced the attacks on the European enclaves of Algiers. The French executed FLN members by guillotine and L'Arbi urged his forces to "shoot down any European, from 18 to 54. No women, no children, no elder." Yacef recalled years later that the Thèbes Road Massacre marked a turning point in the insurgency. Prior FLN attacks had retaliated against mass arrests or executions, the residents of Casbah began to march en masse to the European center of Algiers after Thèbes to avenge their dead. Yacef, in a statesman-like attempt to avoid an all-around bloodbath, barely succeeded in discouraging the confrontation by promising that the FLN would rise to the occasion in due course and time.

Djamila, Zohra, and Hassiba did rise to the occasion on September 30, 1956 by simultaneously bombing a milk bar, a travel agency, and a café frequented by French citizens. And so these three female militant FLN operatives launched the Battle of Algiers. The next month, French military re-directed a Moroccan DC-3 carrying FLN operatives Hocine Aït Ahmed, Ahmed Ben Bella, Mohammed Boudiaf, Mohamed Khider and Mostefa Lacheraf from Rabat to Tunis for a conference with the Sultan of Morocco. French authorities arrested the five upon their unexpected landing in Algiers. In December, former First Indochina War commander at Tonkin, General Raoul Salan, attained the post of Inter Army Commander in Algeria. Salan survived a bazooka assassination attempt the next year, and continued his activities with the *Organisation Armée Secrete*, which eventually led him to a conviction in absentia for treason. Salan initially faced a death penalty, later commuted, and eventually nullified by an act of amnesty.

Mollet next assigned absolute power over all civilian and military matters in Algiers to General Massu in January of 1957. In addition to Massu's 10th Parachute Division, Massu now commanded over 1000 police, the Domestic Intelligence Agency (DST), the external intelligence agency (SDECE), the 11th Parachute Choc Regiment, the 9th Zouave Regiment, the 25th Dragoon Regiment, 55 gendarmes, the mounted 5th *Chasseurs d'Afrique,* and a few thousand other troops from various units.

Prefect Serge Baret signed a delegation of power on January 7, 1957, which ordered as follows:

Over the territory of the Algier department, responsibility for riot control is transferred, from the publication date of this decree, to the military authority that shall exercise police powers normally devoted to civilian authorities.

The decree further required Massu to:

institute zones where stay is regulated or forbidden; to place any person whose activity would prove dangerous to public security and order under house arrest, under surveillance or not; to regulate public meetings, shows, bars; to order declaration of weapons, ammunition and explosives, and order their surrendering or seek and confiscate them; to requisition homes by day or night; to decide of penalties imposed as reparations of damage to public and private property to anyone found to have helped the rebellion in any way.[33]

General Massu, as General Aussaresses had, consistently admitted and defended the use of torture in Algeria; Massu, however, claimed as one additional rationale that he never submitted any captive to any treatment Massu had not first tested on himself. Massu's tactics and methods, humane or otherwise, overcame the FLN in the Casbah and earned him a third star. The victory was merely tactical, though, as the typical colonial brutality of Massu encouraged growing rebellion outside of Algiers, and to some extent internationally. Massu eventually retired with 5 stars, but not without controversy over his protest to the Évian Accords cease fire of 1962, which Massu considered a capitulation to the inferior Algerians and their vanquished FLN. Massu had won the Battle of Algiers.

---

[33] Marie-Monique Robin, *Escadrons de la Mort, L'école Française*, (Paris: Dâecouverte, 2004), 95.

The Évian Accords formally ended the Algerian War with a March 19, 1961 cease-fire and a referendum the next year. The French approved the treaty by 91% and the Algerians by an even higher majority. Charles de Gaulle pronounced Algeria a free and independent country on July 3, 1962, but only after extracting concessions of French influence over the Saharan oil reserves and continued control of French military bases, especially its naval facilities at Mers-el-Kébir, which included underground nuclear testing facilities. The settlement was not without controversy, though, as the hardline OAS expressed their disapproval with a campaign of violence that included a series of bombings and a failed assassination attempt on Charles de Gaulle himself. The real goal of the offensive was to force the FLN to violate the cease-fire and re-ignite the war.

The FLN had managed to resist the OAS as it had survived the French onslaught, contrary to Massu bragging otherwise, and eventually ruled an independent Algeria after the referendum approved the Évian Accords. The FLN, as is often the case, traded its revolutionary status for one party rule after independence; the FLN banned both the *Mouvement National Algérien* (MNA) and the Communist Party of Algeria from participation in government. The liberators, thus, imitated their former oppressors with abrogation of basic freedoms—the freedom to choose political representatives. Consistent with the trichotomy of rebellion, though, the FLN incited the Children of the Casbah to rise up against the French exploitation and minority colonial rule—one of the most insidious forms of class war, often accompanied by genocide. Currently in Algeria the FLN is the largest of three political parties ruling in a coalition government elected in 2007.

Primogeniture and Poverty Pimps

"Whoever oppresses the poor to increase his own wealth, or gives to the rich, will only come to poverty."

—Proverbs 22: 16

The first $5 million of an estate are excluded from inheritance tax, or "death tax" as apologists dysphemize it.

Rise in Exclusion Rate for Estates.

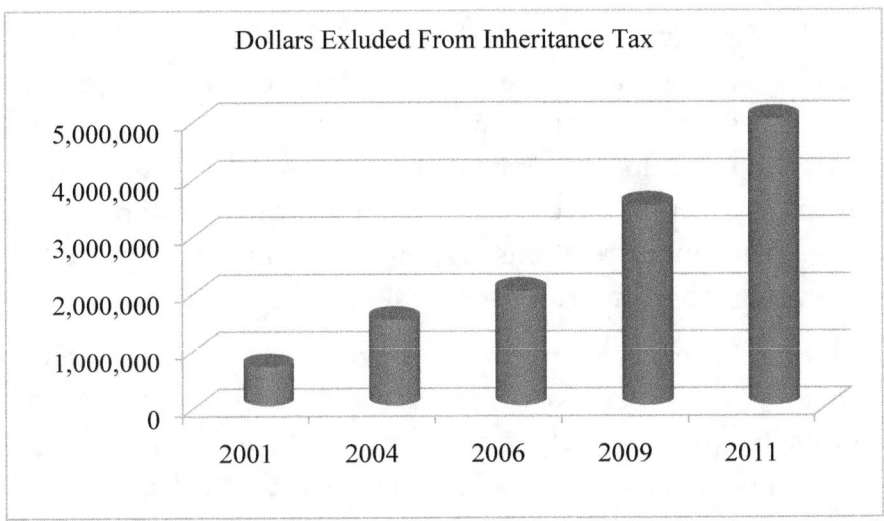

Dollars Exluded From Inheritance Tax

Source: Internal Revenue Service

Rupert Murdoch inherited his first paper from his father, an Oxford grad. Murdoch the junior had directly aided Margaret

Thatcher's breaking of the British mining strike. Murdoch was taking on the unions in his own printing shops at the time, having replaced traditional methods with less labor-intensive lithography. Murdoch laid off 5-thousand union members in 1986. Thatcher had the police take the side of industry, and Murdoch manipulated the other unions, especially the unthreatened reporters, to stand aside. Another of Murdoch's manipulations was to purchase money-losing but influence-producing papers such as *The Sunday Times of London*, which Murdoch uses to curry favor with friendly politicians or punish unfriendly ones, often spying on them by illegal phone tapping, such as was recently revealed in Parliament. Some early statistics include a staggering 25 percent of police investigators on News Corporation's payroll.

Although rival paper *The Guardian* had broken the story earlier, Metropolitan Police continuously pressured the paper to drop the issue. When they did not, the scandal so outraged British sensibilities that Prime Minister David Cameron cancelled his West African vacation to return home and manage the public relations nightmare that included direct involvement by Cameron's senior staff.

A passing of the mantle to Murdoch the third seems likely, given Rupert's octogenarian status and poor public image. The Murdoch empire is likely to survive, though. A recent shareholders meeting at Pebble Beach boasted such an all-star guest list as Bill Clinton, Nicole Kidman, Newt Gingrich, Arnold Schwarzenegger, John McCain, Shimon Perez, and Al Gore. Whatever part of the estate that is subject to United States taxes will enjoy a $5 million dollar exemption and top rate of only 35% of all inheritance over that. Much of Murdoch's current profits derive from the Fox network and news channel that propagandizes working class Americans into subscribing to political positions, such as raising even further the "death tax" exemption, that are entirely contrary to the actual interests of the middle class and working class viewers who contribute to the Murdoch fortune.

The now infamous Koch Brothers of Koch Industries made much of their money from cheating some of the poorest of the poor in America: Native-Americans on reservations. The Koch scheme was to defraud the tribes by cheating them out of 30 to 50 percent of their royalties from oil extraction on reservations. Even the Koch's semi-black sheep brother not involved in the Industries, William, describes billionaire brothers David and Charles Koch as running what William Koch describes as an "organized crime" operation.

To protect their schemes from unwanted regulation or congressional oversight or even investigation, Koch Industries actively support conservative candidates and causes all over the country, including the harsh anti-union initiatives of Scott Walker in Wisconsin and John Kasich in Ohio. It is well known at this point that Koch money helped to found and continue the Tea Party Movement now largely overshadowed by the more organic grass roots Occupy Movement.

CBS' 60 Minutes covered the Koch fraud in the "Blood and Oil and Environmental Negligence" segment first aired in 2000. The story focused on the activities of Koch Industries, which at the time was larger than Dupont, Intel, or Prudential insurance. Unlike those three publicly traded corporations, however, the two brothers own Koch Industries privately.

The next year, 2001, the Bush Administration repealed the "responsible contractor rule" barring historically fraudulent contractors from competing for federal awards.

The following year, 2002, Koch Industries won the contract to supply oil for the nation's Strategic Petroleum Reserve. There were allegations of price fixing and market manipulation associated with the Bush Administration management of the Reserve around the same time.

In 2004 Koch Industries won renewal of the contract.

The corruption and fraud had begun two decades earlier, though, in Oklahoma, where poor reservation residents of the Caddo Tribe noticed their oil royalty checks dropping steadily, but inexplicably, from $3,000 per month to a poverty-level $1,000 per month on national reservation oil wells that yielded millions for Koch Industries.

The United States Senate formed a Special Committee on Investigations under the aegis of the Select Committee on Indian Affairs to inquire. Their 1989 conclusion:

> Koch Oil was engaged in systematic theft,
> stealing millions in Oklahoma alone.

The responsible federal agency, The Bureau of Land Management, had been entirely ineffectual, if not negligent, in enforcing tribal sovereignty and honest accounting of the oil extraction contracts, so the birth privileges of the Koch brothers afforded them almost infinitely greater economic and political advantages than those born and remaining poor on the reservation.

The exploitation continued, though, as reported by *Business Week* in 1996. So blatant was the fraud that the United States Justice Department opened its own investigation. Meanwhile, the Koch brothers enlisted Senator Bob Dole to influence the Senate Special Committee in 1990 to downplay their inquiry. The result, however, was plainly damning:

> Koch Oil, the largest purchaser of Indian oil in the country, is the most dramatic example of an oil company stealing by deliberate mismeasurement and fraudulent reporting.

The report inspired a grand jury probe in 1992 that was eventually dropped, much to the surprise and chagrin of the Senate Special Committee. The Justice Department in 1995 filed $55 million civil suit against Koch Oil for its more than 300 oil spills in the preceding five years. Senator Dole sponsored a bill that served to exonerate the misconduct retroactively. Not coincidentally, the Koch brothers contributed thousands to Dole and other key legislators. One particular legislator was Oklahoma Senator Don Nickles, who sponsored Timothy Leonard for the position of United States Attorney for the district including Oklahoma. Leonard and his family had longtime business ties with the Koch brothers, the Leonards receiving royalty checks for Leonard family wells serviced by Koch Oil. Although there were calls for Leonard to recuse himself from the case for obvious conflict of interest ethics issues, Deputy Attorney General William P. Barr granted Leonard a waiver, and, not surprisingly, Leonard eventually closed the case, terminating the grand jury investigation after 18 months.

The consequences for the obvious corruption? Senator Nickles sponsored Leonard to become a federal judge,

President George H. W. Bush nominated Leonard in November 1991, and the Senate confirmed Leonard in August of 1992.

Meanwhile, hunger, poverty, and lack of health care plague more than 99 percent of the world. United Nations Food and Agriculture Organization registered a spike to over one billion hungry persons in 2009, including twenty million in developing countries. The United States Census Bureau counted over 300,000 Americans living in poverty in 2010. The same year corporate profits in the United States alone rose to $1.7 trillion according to the Commerce Department, and The New York State Comptroller reported that Wall Street found enough gains to offer an *average* bonus of $128,530 to its thousands of financial service industry employees. The State Comptroller began tracking the taxable bonuses in 1985, when the $1.9 billion pool calculated to an average bonus of $13,970.

The pension funds and individual retirement accounts of the working class and middle class managed by the bonus awardees, however, did not fare as well. A 2010 Pew Center report estimated over $1 trillion shortfall in state worker pension funds, some having lost over 50 percent of their value in the 2008 stock market crash. Illinois was the hardest hit with 54 percent lost.

There is more insistence than ever in 2016 on the repeal of all tax loopholes, tax havens, and trade treaties that contribute to the race-to-the-bottom that globalism perpetuates—by design. Taxes on the wealthy have been as high as 93 percent for the top dollars earned. During the boom of the 1990s taxes on corporations and the wealthy were much higher than they are today, yet the economy soared. The Bush tax cuts were second only to the wars in creating the current budget deficits. Does the Sanders presidential campaign signal that it is finally time for the one percent to pay their fair share?

Alma Maters

Comandante Ramona did not die from a bullet, but lack of health care in an ongoing class war in tropical Mexico.

Comandante Ramona was the alma mater of the Chiapas rebellion. The rebel is the alma mater of social change. Then too, we all nourish the rebel, whether we march with the rebel, oppose the rebel, or, by our indifference, create a vacuum for the rebel to fill. We allow a magical semi-realistic incarnation of our nourishing mothers. The Christian Mary, mother of Jesus, we are taught, and some believe, is a virgin. The Mary myth is about hope. Hope is alluring, and hope is free. Revolution is freedom, but it is not free; we often pay for revolution with human blood. The *Comandante* Ramona legend is not about hope; it is about freedom. Thomas Jefferson advised us that a free people must be willing to revolt as often as every generation to cast off any government that does not serve us so that we can replace it with one that does. *Comandante* Ramona's *Ejército Zapatista de Liberación Nacional(EZLN)* fights for the same thing that Sojourner Truth and Geronimo fought for: freedom. Freedom is magical, but it is also real–as real as we are willing to make it.

Home-made signs admonish travelers on Chiapas highways that "ESTA USTED EN TERRITORIO ZAPATISTA EN REBELDIA. AQUI MANDA EL PUEBLO Y EL GOBIERNO OBEDECE." These advisements translate to: "You are now in Zapatista rebel territory. Here, the people rule and the government obeys." This libertarian and local autonomy populism is little different from that of the original Zapatistas of 1910, or the American revolutionaries of 1776. Even the current Tea Party Republicans and their alma mater, Sarah Palin, espouse similar philosophies, perhaps disingenuously. Rebellion and struggle is inherent to humanity. Revolution is as natural as breathing, and is distracted in the United States by means of opiates such as fundamentalist religion, a corporate media cabal, and a debt-fueled consumerism orgy.

On January 8, 1994, *Comandante* Ramona's Zapatistas published *The First Declaration from the Lacandon Jungle*. The Women's Revolutionary Law portion of the manifesto promulgated the following:

1. Women, regardless of their race, creed, color or political affiliation, have the right to participate in the revolutionary struggle in any way that their desire and capacity determine.

2. Women have the right to work and receive a fair salary.

3. Women have the right to decide the number of children they have and care for.

4. Women have the right to participate in the matters of the community and take charge if they are free and democratically elected.

5. Women and their children have the right to primary attention in their health and nutrition.

6. Women have the right to education.

7. Women have the right to choose their partner and are not obliged to enter into marriage.

8. Women have the right to be free of violence from both relatives and strangers.

It is interesting to compare this core document with the United States Constitution, which also asserts freedom and rights for all, except slaves and women. The distinction is stark in places. It is not a coincidence, of course, that the framers of the United States Constitution were (a) men, (b) white, and (c) mostly wealthy. Some also owned slaves, and none other than Thomas Jefferson molested one of his teenage female slaves for years. Jefferson's relationship with the slave girl lasted throughout and after his presidency. DNA testing of descendants of the slave established in 1998 that Jefferson had fathered at least one child with Sally Hemings, whom Jefferson claimed to own as chattel. Unlike the United States Constitution, which condones slavery and largely ignores women as citizens, the Women's Revolutionary Law portion of the *EZLN* declaration of 1994 clearly rejects slavery and demands rights for women, including the right to be free from violence and what we would now refer to as statutory rape, but which Jefferson saw as his property right. Additionally, the opening statement of the *EZLN* declaration of 1994 celebrates a history of struggle against slavery.

The United States Declaration of Independence, largely penned by Thomas Jefferson, begins with a natural law rationale for the separation from Great Britain. The word "men" appears in the famous preamble, which declares them all to be created "equal," but the word "women" appears not once in the entire document. Moreover, of the 56 who signed the founding document of the United States, not one was a woman, a native-American, or an African-American. In contrast, the *EZLN* document expressly includes women, and expressly rejects racism. The inclusion of women was quite natural for the *EZLN* in that nearly one third of their rebel soldiers in 1994 were women.

The Women's Revolutionary Law portion of the *EZLN* declaration of 1994 and the entire *EZLN* document actually more closely resemble the Ten Point Plan of the Black Panther Party than either resemble the United States Declaration of Independence or United States Constitution. The first enumeration in the *EZLN* and Black Panther documents addresses the need for self-determination. The second in each document demands work for each and all. Each document espouses a right to education and health care. And, each document calls for freedom from violence. In fact, the EZLN declaration ends with the following request from the people of Mexico: "...we ask for your participation, your decision to support this plan that struggles for work, land, housing, food, health care, education, independence, freedom, democracy, justice and peace." This list echoes each and every one of the ten points in the 1966 plan of the Black Panther Party.

And although some of have labeled the *EZLN* as Marxists or communists, Engels' 1847 ten-point program of communism features only the demand for education as a single shared point with the demands of *Comandante* Ramona's rebels. Free quality education, however, is an almost obligatory plank in any party platform in any country in the 21st century, so it is difficult to make much of this single similarity in the two documents.

An even more frivolous association has been made between the *EZLN* and Osama Bin Laden. Mexican President Vicente Fox, a Harvard educated neo-liberal, ordered 18,000 troops to the Guatemala border after the attacks of September 11, 2001 ostensibly to prevent Al Qaida from uniting with its Zapatista brethren. Al Qaida, a CIA construct, in fact, never came. The notion that terrorists supposedly Hell-bent on destroying the United States would somehow waste their time and resources in the Mexican rain forest commiserating with peasants struggling for land reform barely rises to the level of laughable. Apparently, Fox did not want to miss his opportunity to jump on the "with us or against us" bandwagon with the "with us."

After promising a withdrawal of soldiers from Chiapas, *Presidente* Fox surreptitiously increased the number of troops in July of 2002. A year after 9/11, *Subcomandante Insurgente* Marcos broke an 18-month silence to congratulate a "big brother" for graduating with honors and launching the subversive magazine *Rebeldia*. The last published words of the *de facto* spokesperson of *EZLN* were: "Democracy! Liberty! Justice!" This mantra closed a letter to *EZLN compañeros* celebrating a 6,000 kilometer protest known as the "Color of the Earth March," which grew and grew from Chiapas to Mexico City. The silence that followed was yet another protest—a protest against broken promises by the "bad government" in Mexico City. The silence was rebellion. The silence was strength. The silence was genius. Fox could do nothing but wait—he knew not how long.

Silence is the weapon of mass affection and first resort of the Women in Black, who protest and memorialize all deaths of all mothers' children in war. The somber power of a Women in Black protest is haunting. One cannot do anything but stop, in awe, and watch for minutes the dark-clad mothers as they throng to exclude the light. Black, too, is the chosen color of the *EZLN* masks of anonymity that *Subcomandante Insurgente*

Marcos describes as dark mirrors of all humanity in protest or rebellion. The Women in Black gather in solidarity with the *EZLN* dead

In 1990, such solidarity aligned several United States trade unions that had grown weary of filing grievances and drafting labor complaints with the federal government. Instead, the unions displayed their political presence not in the courts, but in the streets. Even such hardliner masters of *realpolitik* as Kissinger and Nixon paused when thousands of Americans, "trouble-makers" and all, took to the streets to protest the war in Southeast Asia. Nixon's infamous White House audiotapes reveal that Nixon diminished bombing sorties around the time of protest marches. The marchers literally saved lives of unknown thousands of Cambodians, Laotians, Vietnamese, and even friendly-fired-upon American G.I.s by challenging Nixon's moral and political authority. No doubt *Presidente* Fox heard the ever approaching steps of the Color of the Earth Marchers in 2001 and the ever disquieting silence that haunted the next 18-months

Those in power, in name or in real, often know better than their constituents that the power of a government is a construct—and sometimes a tenuous construct. The key function of a government for the favored is enforcement of property relations and the perpetuation of transfer of wealth up the socioeconomic ladder. The term "class war" is a pair of dirty words to the fortunate, who rarely speak them except to shout down a lower rung citizen who dares to invoke or even suggest redistribution of wealth down the socioeconomic ladder. Secretary of State James Baker for Bush the elder invoked the dirty "class war" term in 2004 when attempting to shout down some Democratic apparatchiks in Ohio who were complaining about Republican businessmen who owned voter-counting machine companies. Some of these same Republican businessmen funded the lobbying for the passage of the NAFTA treaty that served as anti-constitution of the *EZLN*.

Just as the "ghost government" of Madagascar in the 1980s had abandoned certain rural areas nominally under its purview, the Fox administration all but abdicated from ruling Chiapas in any social contract manner of government. In 2000, the election of Fox signaled an end to a one-party system that had misgoverned Mexico for over 70 years. The overtly Catholic and neoliberal National Action Party (PAN) of Fox was just as corrupt as the PRI it had replaced. Worse still, Fox, as a former Coca Cola senior executive, was eager to carve up the Mexican countryside and sell it to the highest transnational corporate bidders—for a small finder's fee.

It was a cross purpose, therefore, to fulfill any of the needs of the people of Chiapas, as they sat on the land that Fox aimed to put up for auction. Why build new schools and clinics to make these human obstacles smart, healthy, or comfortable when what the PAN, Fox, and the transnational corporations wanted was the land and what was beneath it? The people atop the land and its many resources were a living nuisance. Furthermore, Fox would not be alienating any voters, as the Zapatistas rejected voting and would not vote for Fox if they ever changed their collective mind as citizens. But citizens were less than useless to Fox; Fox wanted clients and consumers. Fox was, after all, a trained businessman who sold Coca Cola in the land of the coca leaf and to the descendants of the Incan, Aztec, and Mayan empires. Capitalism chafes at the yoke of democracy. Democracy, however, withers in capitalism. Democracy is about citizens and their needs. Capitalism is about consumers and their desires. The Zapatistas needed and desired their ancestral lands and were willing to fight for them. The Zapatistas were not much as consumers, but they were much more than ordinary citizens, they were rebels.

Fox was an agent of globalism sent to steal the land of the Zapatistas and other *campesinos*, but steal the land legally. The legal scheme was to re-write several articles of the Mexican constitution under the guise of respecting the rights of indigenous peoples while actually cheating them out of their most basic right: the right to land–the land of their ancestors, the land that Emiliano Zapata inspired them to defend in a class war that the Mexican people continue to wage against all odds in Chiapas, Morelos, and Oaxaca.

Ten Points of Praxis

"We be many and they be few."

—Arundhati Roy.

Union wages significantly outpace those of non-union workers.

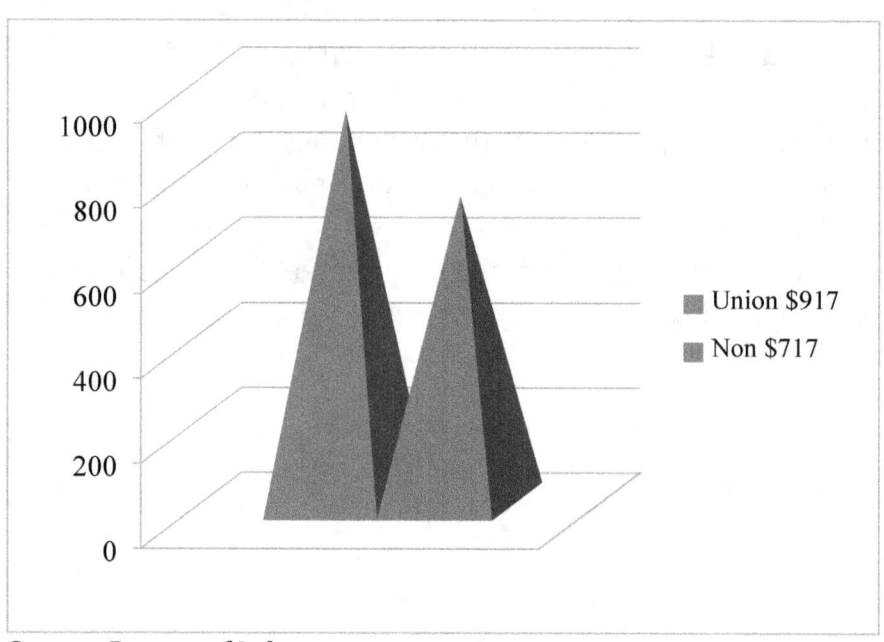

Source: Bureau of Labor

On the eve of the report from the Joint Select Committee on Deficit Reduction, Senator Bernie Sanders and Senator Barbara Mikulski held a press conference urging a continued commitment to the social contract of the New Deal, especially Social Security, which funds itself, despite a very self-serving propaganda campaign to the contrary by Wall Street bankers who want to "manage" the retirement funds for their own profit. Meanwhile, unions are on a steady decline, falling from 35 percent of the workforce after World War II to less than 12 percent in 2011, mostly in the government sector. One of the many benefits of union membership is higher wages. Also of concern is the $50 billion plus spent on military intelligence, more than spent federally on public education or public health.

So, what to do?

How do the ninety-nine percent join their movements like simple organisms coming together, "graxing" their individually small but collectively significant power, to overcome the hierarchical structure created and exploited by the elites? Simple life forms create communities to overcome problems that they could only address together what educators refer to as praxis.

What is our progressive praxis, then?

Senator Mikulski suggests a good first starting point: end the extremely costly wars of aggression in Iraq and Afghanistan, bring the troops home, and keep them here, defending the homeland, not attacking, invading, or occupying someone else's homeland, and spend that money on rebuilding America's roads, bridges, schools, airports, harbors, libraries, and parks with American workers. Our war machine is and has been "the greatest purveyor of violence in the" world's history, to quote Dr. Martin Luther King, Jr. We must insist on a much smaller military budget, which currently accounts for half of all discretionary spending and outpaces all other countries' military budgets combined. War spending and the inequitable

Bush tax cuts are the primary causes of the current budget deficits.

Here are nine other steps we can take:

2.   Discuss politics and economics with your family, neighbors, co-workers and engage in electoral politics—as a beginning not an end. Remind all who will listen that the United States is a constitutional republic that grants only those powers to the government that are listed in the constitution itself, one of which is the power—and the duty—to "provide for the general welfare" of the citizenry.

3.   Support unions and work-place regulation, including—primarily—collective bargaining rights. Do not cross picket lines; boycott businesses that mistreat workers. Establish a union at your work place if it is not union protected currently. If it is, read your contract, attend your union meetings, and enforce your contract.

4.   Re-instate Glass-Steagall and similar banking regulation, including banning derivatives as well as the now entirely legal insider trading of United States senators and representatives. The banking and finance industry—especially the "too big to fail" houses, do not have America's interests in mind when they gamble on risky investments, knowing that they can go to the congress they have bought and paid for to insist on favorable legislation to save them from their own misdeeds. This must stop. In the meantime, we should all hold our savings in local, community institutions that will invest our money in local projects instead of gambling our money in the derivatives market that are all too prevalent instruments held by larger banks.

5. Participate in Occupy and other protests while rejecting police-state tactics and practices. Visit the nearest Occupy site or start your own locally. If you go, bring a video recorder or phone to document any police misconduct. If you record any such, share it with the media, mainstream and independent, and the local and federal authorities, including the FBI. The ACLU distributes a free cell phone app, Mobile Justice, that forwards your video immediately to the ACLU.

6. Pass a Constitutional Amendment: (a) establishing nationally funded elections, (b) stripping personhood from corporations, (c) asserting that money is not speech, (d) prohibiting all foreign military action not prior approved by a supermajority of the American people by popular vote, (e) abolishing the Federal Reserve, and (f) subjecting congress to all laws, such as insider trading or sexual harassment prohibitions, that congress imposes on the citizenry.

7. Fight for full funding of: (a) public education, (b) infrastructure projects such as roads, bridges, and public buildings, (c) Medicare, (d) the National Science Foundation, (e) the National Aeronautic and Space Administration, (f) the National Institute of Health, and (g) all other programs that "provide for the general welfare, " of the people. Also, reject any attempts to diminish or privatize Social Security. The surest and simplest way to ensure the long-term solvency of what many Americans consider to be the most successful and popular government "entitlement" program is to remove the cap on the income subject to Social Security taxation, currently any income over $110,100. There is no economic or moral reason to exempt income over this amount from a levy; it is merely another gift to the wealthiest Americans, most of whom

expect to, or already do, benefit from Social Security. These are programs that need increased funding. They are the solution. Austerity will only deepen the current recession by reducing spending power of the middle class that drives the economy.

8.   Demand immigration reform that respects human dignity, family unity, and the natural act of migration, thus rejecting the concept of a person being "illegal." Immigrants created this country, and allowing their mistreatment lowers wages for all and condones police-state tactics in our communities at a cost that we cannot afford any more than the state penal systems currently incarcerating over 2 million Americans.

9.   Attend every civic event you possibly can, run for an office, and monitor the mainstream press, writing to the editor or ombudsman when the coverage is lacking, misleading, or biased. Democracy works best with maximum participation at all times in all ways. The lobbyists are thousands strong and do not take breaks between elections, so neither can we.

10. Insist on the repeal of all tax loopholes, tax havens, and trade treaties, such as TPP, that contribute to the race-to-the-bottom that globalism perpetuates—by design. Taxes on the wealthy have been as high as 93 percent for the top dollars earned. During the boom of the 1990s taxes on corporations and the wealthy were much higher than they are today, yet the economy soared. The Bush tax cuts were second only to the wars in creating the current budget deficits. It is time for the one percent to pay their fair share.

Acknowledgments

Thanks to all writers, educators, jurists, politicians, activists, and citizens who fight for freedom and equality. Special thanks to Professors Sterling, Phillip, and Hermelinda and Judge Ruth.

About the author

Eric Michael Moberg is the author of three novels: *Big Noise at the Funky Butt Jass Club*, *Cowboys and Scumbags*, and *End of Summer*. He teaches composition, literature, logic, rhetoric, and business communication at City College of San Francisco, Diablo Valley College, and San Francisco State University.

See his author page at:

www.amazon.com/Eric-MichaelMoberg/e/B00J8WR7KM

See his scholarship at:

https://sfsu.academia.edu/EricMoberg